Teaching English Today
Advocating Change in the Secondary Curriculum
BARRIE R.C. BARRELL, ROBERTA F. HAMMETT,
JOHN S. MAYHER, and GORDON M. PRADL, Editors

Bridging the Literacy Achievement Gap,
Grades 4–12
DOROTHY S. STRICKLAND and
DONNA ALVERMANN, Editors

Crossing the Digital Divide:
Race, Writing, and Technology in the Classroom
BARBARA MONROE

Out of this World: Why Literature Matters to Girls
HOLLY VIRGINIA BLACKFORD

Critical Passages:
Teaching the Transition to College Composition
KRISTIN DOMBEK and
SCOTT HERNDON

Making Race Visible:
Literary Research for Cultural Understanding
STUART GREENE and
DAWN ABT-PERKINS, Editors

The Child as Critic: Developing Literacy through
Literature, K–8, FOURTH EDITION
GLENNA SLOAN

Room for Talk: Teaching and Learning in a
Multilingual Kindergarten
REBEKAH FASSLER

Give Them Poetry!
A Guide for Sharing Poetry with Children K–8
GLENNA SLOAN

The Brothers and Sisters Learn to Write: Popular
Literacies in Childhood and School Cultures
ANNE HAAS DYSON

"Just Playing the Part": Engaging Adolescents in
Drama and Literacy
CHRISTOPHER WORTHMAN

The Testing Trap: How State Writing Assessments
Control Learning
GEORGE HILLOCKS, JR.

The Administration and Supervision of Reading
Programs, THIRD EDITION
SHELLEY B. WEPNER, DOROTHY S. STRICKLAND,
and JOAN T. FEELEY, Editors

School's Out! Bridging Out-of-School Literacies
with Classroom Practice
GLYNDA HULL and KATHERINE SCHULTZ, Editors

Reading Lives: Working-Class Children and
Literacy Learning
DEBORAH HICKS

Inquiry Into Meaning: An Investigation of Learning
to Read, REVISED EDITION
EDWARD CHITTENDEN and TERRY SALINGER,
with ANNE M. BUSSIS

"Why Don't They Learn English?" Separating Fact
from Fallacy in the U.S. Language Debate
LUCY TSE

Conversational Borderlands: Language and Identity
in an Alternative Urban High School
BETSY RYMES

Inquiry-Based English Instruction
RICHARD BEACH and JAMIE MYERS

The Best for Our Children: Critical Perspectives on
Literacy for Latino Students
MARÍA DE LA LUZ REYES and
JOHN J. HALCÓN, Editors

Language Crossings:
Negotiating the Self in a Multicultural World
KAREN L. OGULNICK, Editor

What Counts as Literacy?
Challenging the School Standard
MARGARET GALLEGO and
SANDRA HOLLINGSWORTH, Editors

Critical Encounters in High School English:
Teaching Literary Theory to Adolescents
DEBORAH APPLEMAN

Beginning Reading and Writing
DOROTHY S. STRICKLAND and
LESLEY M. MORROW, Editors

Reading for Meaning:
Fostering Comprehension in the Middle Grades
BARBARA M. TAYLOR, MICHAEL F. GRAVES, and
PAUL VAN DEN BROEK, Editors

Writing in the Real World
ANNE BEAUFORT

Young Adult Literature and the
New Literary Theories
ANNA O. SOTER

Literacy Matters: Writing and Reading the Social Self
ROBERT P. YAGELSKI

Building Family Literacy in an Urban Community
RUTH D. HANDEL

Children's Inquiry:
Using Language to Make Sense of the World
JUDITH WELLS LINDFORS

Engaged Reading:
Processes, Practices, and Policy Implications
JOHN T. GUTHRIE and
DONNA E. ALVERMANN, Editors   *(Continued)*

TEACHING ENGLISH TODAY

Advocating Change
in the Secondary Curriculum

Barrie R. C. Barrell
Roberta F. Hammett
John S. Mayher
Gordon M. Pradl
EDITORS

Foreword by Patrick Shannon

Teachers College, Columbia University
New York and London

Published by Teachers College Press, 1234 Amsterdam Avenue, New York, NY 10027

Library of Congress Cataloging-in-Publication Data

Teaching English today : advocating change in the secondary curriculum / Barrie R. C.
   Barrell . . . [et al.] editors ; foreword by Patrick Shannon.
      p. cm. — (Language and literacy series)
   Includes bibliographical references and index.
   ISBN 0-8077-4478-6 (cloth) — ISBN 0-8077-4477-8 (pbk.)
      1. English language—Study and teaching (Secondary)—United States. 2. English
   language—Study and teaching (Secondary)—Canada. 3. Language arts (Secondary)—
   Curricula—United States. 4. Language arts (Secondary)—Curricula—Canada. I. Barrell,
   Barrie R. C. (Barrie Robert Christopher), 1946– II. Language and literacy series (New York,
   N.Y.)

   LB1631.T283 2004
   428′.0071′273—dc22

                                                                          2004043966

ISBN 0-8077-4477-8 (paper)
ISBN 0-8077-4478-6 (cloth)

Printed on acid-free paper

Manufactured in the United States of America

11   10   09   08   07   06   05   04   8   7   6   5   4   3   2   1

Contents

Foreword

These are dangerous times for English teachers. While waiting in a hotel lobby at the American Educational Research Association convention in Chicago recently, I eavesdropped on a conversation between two professors who had just completed a session on the production of secondary school English teachers.

"I agree with you about content," offered the first.
"Students must get a handle on the structure of any discipline," replied the second. "And we can help them with that."
"But those damn reading people insist that it's a literacy issue."
"After decoding, there's nothing but literature to learn in reading. Writing's just a matter of content."
"Yes, and there's not much to literature any more. Not with what they teach now. Since there are no classic works, what is there to teach?"
"It's all a waste of time. No underlying structures—no standards worth the effort."

This dialogue left me cold. Two professors erase a century-old field with a few declarative sentences and then move on to other matters. In their eyes, English fails to measure up as an academic discipline with an easily identifiable internal structure. Composition is simply a matter of knowing what you want to write. Reading is recognizing words and understanding the structure of various genres. Knowledge of literature is blocked by the critiques of the canon. What is left of English education in their eyes is "a waste of time." Living through the debacle over national standards for English language arts in the United States, I am steeled to withstand the tired debates over hard and soft disciplines. The subversion of the postmodern turn, however, rattled my usual quick dismissal of traditionalism. By accepting the limits of the canon and spreading writing across the curriculum, these professors eliminated any need to continue teaching English in secondary schools. Think about it—no study of language and how it works, no study of text and how it positions us, and no study of representations and what they can do to and for our identities.

In this book, Barrell, Hammett, Mayher, and Pradl meet the old and new challenges to English education head on. They've assembled a celebrated group of educators and researchers who take up the issues of text, reading, writing, culture, knowledge, and history. They build their cases theoretically, practically, and politically. I choose the word *cases* carefully because the contributors do not always agree on what the problems are or which solutions should be attempted. That is one of the strengths of the book. While readers will not find dialogues like the one I overheard among these chapters, they are treated to a wide range of positions on the value of and the values in various iterations of English curricula. The tensions among these positions are generative.

Consider the decision to split the chapters evenly between contributors from Canada and from the United States. Canada has recently centralized educational planning beyond the provincial level to four national regions in order to bring education more closely under national scrutiny and to cut costs. Yet the English curricula from these centers are often progressive, at least in terms of their consideration of multiple sign systems and cultural studies. At the moment, English curricula in the United States are still negotiated locally. However, the federal government's use of high-stakes testing in order to turn schools into markets for commercial textbook and test publishers has a centralizing tendency that has curtailed English educators' efforts to engage students' lives in their instruction. The contributors to this volume explore the limits and possibilities of both organizational structures and many other such tensions, paying particular attention to students not well served in schools today and posing new projects for readers to consider.

Armed with these arguments, English teachers are better prepared to enter debates about the purpose and value of English education. Through discussions of the issues raised in these chapters, teachers learn much more than how to defend their ground. The contributors push beyond the barriers that stand between current practices and new possibilities; some of the barriers are constructed for English teachers and others are within English teachers. This book asks readers to work on their field and themselves simultaneously, which might benefit those two professors.

Patrick Shannon
Pennsylvania State University

Introduction

BARRIE R. C. BARRELL AND ROBERTA F. HAMMETT
Memorial University of Newfoundland

JOHN S. MAYHER AND GORDON M. PRADL
New York University

THE CONTEXT FOR THIS TEXT

The real impetus for this collection came shortly after 9/11 when Canada rallied to help its southern neighbor. Ambulance and fire personnel from Quebec and Ontario drove through the night to New York City. Seventy-nine transatlantic planes landed in Newfoundland and Labrador, Canada's most eastern province, and their occupants were quickly billeted among the small towns and villages of the province. Good neighbors, it was said, were doing only what good neighbors do. Later, the Rockerfeller Foundation, in gratitude for the kindness shown to three of its executives, donated new computer equipment to a Newfoundland school that had provided e-mail access for them during the extended stopover. A doctor matched the donations of his fellow passengers and set up a university scholarship for students in the small town where they had been housed. Picking up this spirit, the four of us felt a renewed energy to reexamine English language arts education. If we could commingle the voices of neighbors and friends from both sides of the 49th parallel, then perhaps this would contribute to our understanding of the new imperatives that mark the work we do as teachers of English.

The chapters in this book, if anything, show that English language arts (ELA) in our countries have much in common. As teacher educators, we are struggling with a discipline in metamorphosis. We desire our subject to be enabling, to cross borders of dialect and linguistic privilege, and to speak more directly to the human spirit, while evoking a sense of social justice that is needed to keep this spirit free. We wish the voices of the Caribbean and the Asian and African diasporas to intermingle with those traditional voices that have held places of privilege in our schools. We want new genres and technologies to facilitate the expression of plural voices and expand the possibilities of communication.

To do so requires that we acknowledge the globalization of the publishing, communications, information, media, and entertainment industries and their profound impact on English language arts education. It also requires that we take seriously the circumstances under which public education struggles to operate. We are mindful of the neighborhoods of the inner city and acknowledge those who live in the isolation of far northern spaces. We see the increased use of technology in the workplace and in the daily lives of citizens on both sides of the border. We appreciate the ever-increasing diversity of school populations in urban centers such as Los Angeles, Vancouver, Chicago, Toronto, New York, Montreal, Calgary, and Miami, and in the less populated areas of the Midwest, the South, the Prairies, and the Atlantic Provinces. Acknowledging school diversity is important in the reconstruction of a new vision of literacy for our children. While there is a need for a flexible and technologically proficient workforce, we want to assert that students need to feel comfortable moving about in digital formats and contexts, even as they do so critically.

Canada and the United States understandably have their differences. Because this collection is published in the United States, the Canadian editors have yielded to the use of American Standard English, including its spelling conventions. Further, the American editors, following the precedent of Beverly Daniel Tatum (1999, p. 15), decided to capitalize Black and White in all instances involving people or language so as to avoid establishing a "marked" versus an "unmarked" usage distinction.

There are other differences. For instance, jurisdictional consolidations have left Canada with four large regional consortia controlling its curricula (Ontario, Quebec, the western and territorial region, and the Atlantic region). Centralized planning in Canada means devising curricula for huge geographical areas. The United States, on the other hand, appears to rely more heavily on local authorities and individual states to guide curricular decisions in ELA. Still, as the late Jim Moffett pointed out at the International Federation for the Teaching of English (IFTE) conference in Ottawa in 1986, curriculum in the United States is actually dictated by the conglomerate publishers who are increasingly controlled by politicized textbook-selection committees from Texas, California, and Florida. Centralized power means that particular interest groups, ministries of education, or school boards have less leverage and this leaves broad national goals and global perspectives to be articulated by policy makers who are often far removed from the local scene. As Canada struggles to find its place in the globalized economy, its vision of an overarching economic imperative demands a price: The immediate needs of the Pacific or Atlantic fishing village, the prairie farming community, or the isolated native communities are too easily neglected.

Centralization has seemingly made it easier to construct language and literacy philosophies. The new Canadian secondary ELA frameworks deemphasize the reading of canonical works, increase the types of texts and literatures to be read, include media education at all levels, write the use of technology directly into learning outcome statements, and broaden the variety of ways students might compose and represent knowledge and information, including hypermedia, illustration, dance, drama, photography, and computer graphics. These frameworks, however, continue to link the development of standard Canadian English, first and foremost, to statements of literacy competence for individual students.

Throughout, the new Canadian curricula documents encourage group or cohort productions and representations, yet in doing so it surrenders its former conception of literacy as an individual possession and/or performance. Adopting shared conceptions are clearly important, but they carry a certain risk: Student difference and uniqueness can too easily be ignored. Such conceptions of shared student literacy occur most often in the curriculum documents when media or computer-mediated text creation, exchange, and display are engaged. Sharing text production by students can be linked to the postindustrial information economy's workplace requirement for team approaches to or virtual experiences with problem solving and knowledge production. While this trend toward technologizing of literacy is grounded in Canada's rapid integration into global markets and encouraged by the so-called requirements of transnational business mandates, there are often unexamined consequences regarding how social resources become misallocated and how the social agency of citizens can be diminished.

Canonical British, American, and Canadian literatures—the mainstays of many provincial secondary English education programs—and traditional ways of writing now share space with new media constructions, visual texts, and the silicon-based technologies of electronic composing, electronic information transfer networks, and Web texts. Curriculum planners mandated the use of technology in all aspects of the English language arts curriculum. Writing is now seen as but one of many ways to engage and represent textual information or artistic creations.

In contrast, the standards movement, and its reification in high-stakes testing, has made written literacy even more central than ever in the United States. In New York, for example, no one can now graduate from high school without passing a Regents Examination, which includes four separate essays, written in two 3-hour sessions. One is prompted by a text presented orally, but reading and writing are clearly the core language arts abilities being tested. Further, in the recent revision of the New York standards for teacher certification, two courses in language and literacy—reading and writing—were mandated for *all* teacher candidates.

While some U.S. constituencies do encourage computer applications in the English classroom and do view media literacy as a part of the curriculum, their inclusion varies from school district to school district. In Canada, the use of computers and the inclusion of media studies within individual schools still come down to the availability of costly computers, Internet access, and materials and supplies. However, at the provincial and territorial level these new literacies and their accompanying skills are written directly into the guiding documents; they are no longer ad hoc appendages to English language arts programs. Their presence gives direct support to those teachers of English who incorporate technology into their classes, but this also means pushing more traditional teachers to begin viewing English education as a discipline in the midst of change—a discipline where texts and textual engagements are shifting in light of different entertainment patterns, reading habits, and communications requirements.

The idea for this book arose out of this shifting vision for secondary English language arts and an evolving view of literacy. The text asked a broad and inclusive group of practitioner-researchers to express thinking about various current issues in secondary English education. Not all the contributors support the changes taking place in the English language arts curriculum. All would agree, however, that to support, resist, or partially accept a changing vision of what might occur in the ELA classroom requires some understanding of the history, intentions, and practices of our dynamic discipline. Willinsky (Chapter 2) and Pradl and Mayher (Chapter 1) address the role that recent history plays in the positioning of language and communications. They also acknowledge the many schools on both sides of the border where immigrant populations and previously underserved students bring diverse voices, dialects, genres, and cultural experiences to English class.

Many changes in our discipline have been occurring while new preservice teachers of English have been in college and university, and in-service teachers have been struggling with a myriad of other professional challenges and educational policy changes. In Newfoundland and Labrador, these challenges and changes include New Pathways, a policy of inclusion of students with special needs, and the reorganization of the denominational public school system to eliminate religious affiliations. In Ontario, the elimination of Grade 13 is creating changes in both school and university courses. In British Columbia, transformations include increasing numbers of ESL students and non-English speakers in classrooms.

In New York there are schools where more than a hundred languages are spoken and where a significant achievement gap exists between the fortunate and the poor, even as public resources are diverted in other directions (Robert Tobias, personal communication, April 2000). This achievement gap is widening for both African Americans and Latinos as measured by standardized test scores, which seem to be the only measure anyone in power recognizes these days. And, in what strikes us as a vicious cycle, the "low-achieving" schools get mandated a standardized, more or less teacher-proof curriculum. This probably means that the gap will only increase. Yet, even stranger, if improvement does not occur in some timely fashion, authorities are threatening to take funding away from "failing" schools, rather than turn the spotlight on the various inequities that comprise a "failing" social system, inequities which are much more widespread than those authorities want to admit. Per pupil expenditure, for instance, differs greatly depending upon the wealth of the school district. Those in control more and more support quick fixes and regulations for problems that continue to be extremely intractable. Furthermore, in the tradition of privatization and outsourcing, the U.S. trend is to hire noneducator managers to run the schools. In short, it seems unlikely that thoughtful alternatives, even ones that are not necessarily more costly, will be pursued under the current administration.

Bobbi Hammett's reflections on becoming an English teacher parallel those of many of us. The path she followed is similar to the experiences of Gordon, John, and Barrie, and she demonstrates the distances we have all traveled since we first entered the classroom decades ago.

ADJUSTING TO CHANGE: BOBBI'S PERSPECTIVE

As a high school student who enjoyed the romance of literature (as Kelly describes in Chapter 4) and who decided to go on to a small liberal arts college to continue to enjoy both English and history en route to becoming an English teacher, I faced few challenges to my thinking about English as a discipline and how to teach it. My education experiences confirmed this: No one asked me— as McClay (Chapter 6) and Dickar (Chapter 5) do in this volume—to approach teaching writing in a way different from my learning experiences; in fact, other than academic essays about aspects of teaching and learning, I wrote little, and produced nothing that then would have been considered "creative." I continued to read the canon, was introduced to all the "great works" through a series of survey courses: British literature in three time divisions, drama throughout history, Shakespeare, Canadian and American literature, the novel from its development into the twentieth century, and so on. These courses confirmed that reading was a process of understanding the author's intended meaning and appreciating the aesthetic nature of the works. Interpretive works by great critics urged my reading along: They told me what I was reading and I comfortably integrated their readings with mine, or, to be more precise, subordinated my responses to the "correct response." No one invited me to consider what was going on in my world the day of my reading, so there was no reason to understand how those contexts influenced the particular meanings I was negotiating with the text. No one suggested, as Kynard (Chapter 7) does, that meanings might be discourse dependent, contested, or intimately tied up in the multiple identities of individual students. No one asked me to learn or teach media, as Mackey (Chapter 8) does, let alone speaking, listening, or computer technology.

In those days no World Wide Web was in sight, and therefore no plethora of sites about authors from many different nations and cultures for me to investigate. There was no challenge for me to view my subject from a cultural studies perspective or engage in multidisciplinary and political or cultural practices and investigations with students, as Morgan (Chapter 3) suggests. Teacher education classes, teachers' manuals, and curriculum guides told me flat out how to teach and gave me sample lesson plans and outlined "successful" approaches to teaching Shakespeare and canonical authors. I was never encouraged to question the existing curricula nor to deliberately critique subject English itself as Willinsky (Chapter 2), Morgan (Chapter 3), and Kelly (Chapter 4) do.

Yet I started teaching. The teachers' guides and prepackaged questions about the literature that I found in the bookroom served to prop me up. Occasionally, I interrupted my literature lessons to teach some grammar and composition, so that my students might more "correctly" write the essays about literature I was assigning them. I even consulted my own high school notebooks for teaching ideas; frequently I repeated stories about authors I had read and heard during my university courses. Sometimes I appealed to those who controlled the school and department budgets to see if they would supplement the texts that had been used for years. But what did I have my eye on? *New works*, which had been my favorites from university days.

I didn't integrate texts or genres much, except as this already occurred in thematic chapters of anthologies, and certainly I didn't think texts might "speak" to one another. I did not assume that students might read a variety of texts instead of one class text or that much knowledge would be transferred from unit to unit. Occasionally, on exams, I would ask students to develop intertextual themes, but I did not think of interconnecting a variety of reading and writing and collaborating practices of the kind Morgan (Chapter 3) suggests. I did not have the insights Kelly (Chapter 4) offers. I thought I had to be the teacher, set the direction of the class, lead and stay in tight control of the discussions. Students could make presentations but not direct their own learning or that of their peers.

Knowledge also used to be so certain—someone else or some text had it and transmitted it to me as a learner. I processed it so that I had it too and could then transmit it to someone else, like my students. To make sure they learned it was simple: I tested them, not only requiring them to regurgitate it, but also to synthesize and interpret and integrate it. But I never really considered that I—or *they*, for that matter—had any role in its production. And I did not think about assessment and evaluation in the ways that Beck (Chapter 10) suggests, as she encourages us to reconsider our ideas about the purposes and means of assessing the competencies and achievements of our students.

My point in these reflections is to emphasize the complexities of teaching high school English language arts that this text seeks to explicate. Of course, the teaching of English has always been a complex, challenging endeavor. English teachers who cared about meeting the very diverse needs of students in their classrooms have always struggled with questions of inclusion and exclusion—both of curriculum materials and differently abled students. There were always students in our classes who did not relate to or appreciate the texts we had selected for close examination, and we tried to address those issues. We have gradually incorporated more and more media texts into our courses and, along with this, have integrated the many technologies, from video cameras and desktop publishing programs to audiotapes and even in-house broadcasting suites.

Together English teachers have been busy remaking our subject; for not only do the new curricula emerge from national and international social, economic, and political forces, they also emanate from our struggles in classrooms. Curricula emerge from our attempts to make sense of our practice, our desire to make our classrooms better places for more students, our need to solve the daily issues that arise in our schools, and our urge to respond to those complex forces that are felt at the local level and are the context of each and every classroom and school.

OUR DISCIPLINE TURNED UPSIDE DOWN: JOINING A CRITICAL DIALOGUE

This book is about rethinking our subject and, in fact, reproducing our subject—English. It is about rethinking our practice—both what and how we teach on both sides of the border. We begin with the name of our discipline. By adding "language arts" we indicate a change in emphasis from literature to all the arts related to language: oracy, visual literacy, media literacy, grammar and composition, and information and communication technologies.

Chapters in this collection reconceptualize knowledge, asking, What is knowledge? Where does it come from? Rather than information that is pre-packaged by experts and transmitted from teachers and textbooks, knowledge includes understandings that are socially constructed by students themselves in self-directed inquiries. Knowledge is generated in a process that involves reading transactions and other ways of receiving information, such as personal experiences, observations, sharing and critical dialogue, and creative, active enterprises of all kinds.

And curriculum seems to have changed. No longer does it proscriptively name texts or delineate themes and content for study as preparation for exams that are mandated and administered by province or state. Now curricula speak of outcomes and talk about interwoven strands. The new curricula offer new conceptions of literacy influenced in part by the integration of media studies and computer technologies in ELA curricula. Defining literacy used to be so simple—reading and writing. Now, as Morgan (Chapter 3), Mackey (Chapter 8), Hammett (Chapter 9), and Pradl and Mayher (Chapter 1) demonstrate, traditional texts are being decentered and a wider variety of new kinds of texts are taking their place and demanding the implementation of a whole range of different text practices.

This collection challenges us to reconceptualize evaluation as Beck (Chapter 10) does, reconsidering its purpose and value. Such reconsiderations bring into question the nature and purposes of schooling itself! Dickar (Chapter 5) and McClay (Chapter 6) would have us re-envision writing pedagogy, insisting that new technologies, different genres, and alternative teaching practices and orientations be investigated and accommodated and implemented when appropriate. Mackey (Chapter 8) invites us to interrogate our interpretations of texts, by identifying the values and assumptions that underlie different readings and in turn pursuing the consequences of any given reading and the blind spots it might reveal.

Together we might discover and investigate threads of meaning that provide the intertextual links among all these chapters, noting where the ideas and concepts privileged in "official" curricular documents originated and how they are fleshed out or argued in descriptions of the practices of assessment, reading, writing, speaking, and viewing that each author presents. And most importantly, we note that similar destinations can be reached by traveling different routes through this book. By discussing and exploring the beliefs and assumptions about knowledge, literacy, and schooling that underlie this activity, that question, or any particular theory advocated here, we keep open the lively and often contentious dialogue that for years has characterized our profession of reflective practitioners. Accordingly, the historical periods that Willinsky (Chapter 2) delineates are reinvented as the discourses that Kelly (Chapter 4) describes.

In this book we raise pertinent questions about mandated curricula, high-stakes testing, conventional teaching practices, and the mechanical preparation of ELA arts teachers. Clearly, new curricula should be read critically: Whose interests are being served and whose are not? What may be their effects on various constituents? What perspectives, theories, and ideas are privileged and which are ignored? So many questions to ask, so many issues not yet addressed. Accordingly, we invite and indeed welcome critique of the various propositions put forward in this book. In her chapter, for example, Hammett enthusiastically endorses the use of computer technology in schools with little questioning of the negative aspects or potentially harmful effects on the quality of life of aboriginal and other peoples and their cultures. Her chapter does not address the race, class, gender, and ability inequities that characterize access to and use of computers. Nor does it mention that the costs of computer technology will likely be taken from library book budgets. Still, consider what wonders are possible, when an electronic copy of *Romeo and Juliet* can be downloaded from the Internet for use in hypermedia composing and other activities—including reading or editing for theatrical production—thus saving the cost of purchasing a print copy.

If, as a profession, English teachers are to retain a respectful authority over our discipline, it is crucial that we not accept uncritically any mandates or standards set by new curricula, whether they originate locally, or in the state, province, or territory. For, as with this book, numerous essential issues remain unaddressed in the curricula. For example, mandates generally fail to take a stand on the inclusion of works by lesbian and gay writers, surely an issue of interest to secondary ELA teachers and their students. They are also silent when it comes to matters of censorship. Presumably, departments of education still expect teachers to choose books appropriate to the moral principles and social values of their local communities. But doesn't this effectively maintain the status quo, forcing teachers to censor books rather than defend their choices against irate parents and unsupportive school boards? Similarly, new curricula provide no solution to the pervasive power and influence of mass media and mass communications and their concomitant threat to traditional languages. Wherever English functions as a vital subject in the classroom, it serves to stir up issues such as these that must be debated; unfortunately, curricular documents and standards movements seldom invite such active reflection. Thus we hold this collection up against apathy, docility, and defeat, hoping the searching words of the assembled authors provoke controversy and stimulate thinking on both sides of our common border.

REFERENCE

Tatum, B. D. (1999). *"Why are all the Black kids sitting together in the cafeteria?" and other conversations about race*. New York: Basic Books.

CHAPTER 1

Chat Room Musings: English Teaching in a Changing World

GORDON M. PRADL AND JOHN S. MAYHER
New York University

Gordon: Okay, John, let's get on with this chapter. The other day you made an important point about how drastically circumstances have changed since our generation came on the scene as English teachers.

John: Yes, we have to begin by admitting that collectively we've been teaching English and teaching English teachers for more than 80 years. In the 1960s there seemed to be a secure and complete vision of education in place. Even after Sputnik, we knew why we were in the classroom, and in part it was to help kids become like us. This meant everything from enjoying and reading literature critically to learning grammar and the rules for correct writing. Of course, television was becoming very present in our lives, and the 1960s themselves were opening up a Pandora's box of social concern and activism—seemingly the authority of every institution was being challenged. Still, there really wasn't all that much confusion about what should be going on in English classes.

Gordon: That's right. Those of us who entered teacher education did so with a clear image of what being an "English teacher" means—and that's a literature teacher. We thought our own experiences as readers of literature should serve as a guide for what we promoted in our pupils. When we first got into this game, the dominant mode of literature teaching, and literary criticism, was New Criticism, and we were urged by such notables as the Commission on English (1965) to turn our charges into New

Critics. The key to New Criticism was context-free "close" reading, which focused on the text in isolation and was built on the belief that it was possible to establish and then preach a "correct" reading.

John: Regurgitation even back then! From today's perspective it's now easy to see the pernicious effect of that approach and mind-set. It served to create generations of students who believed that only teachers had the secret keys to unlock the hidden meanings of literature. No need to read yourself, since you were likely to be "wrong," and might as well wait for the teacher to tell you what it meant. Only a fool would be oblivious to knowing that would be expected on the test! And better yet, there were *Cliffs Notes.*

Gordon: But the shifts in literary theory during the past decades have provided a good example of how theory does impact classroom practice. Louise Rosenblatt's (1938/1995) transactional theory began it in 1938, but she was never fully recognized until decades later when others suddenly become aware of the importance of "reader response." A "transactional approach" to teaching English recognizes that the student, whether as reader or as writer, has an important role to play in any lesson.

John: Certainly, actual flesh-and-blood readers had for a long time been the missing ingredient in how meaning making actually occurs in the process of literary reading. Later theoretical developments including structuralism, poststructuralism, deconstruction, postmodernism and the like have all provided different models of reading to emulate. So too have the emphases of feminism, cultural studies, ethnic studies, and others, which bring still further perspectives to the literature classroom.

Gordon: And all of this forced us to recognize that the teaching, and reading, of literature is never context-free. It is always a politically significant act. This means teachers must consider their own pedagogical stance within that political context as I have explored in considering teaching literature in a democratic context and reading as a social act (Pradl, 1996).

John: Of course, once the reader and the context became acknowledged then the genie was out of the bottle, so to speak. You couldn't any longer ignore the fact that your students might naturally come up with literary interpretations different from yours.

Gordon: In fact, you could even say that if they weren't there was something wrong, like maybe you weren't allowing them to speak up and find their own voice.

John: But returning to the legacy of the 1960s—when we discovered a whole lot of new voices clamoring to be heard—you could say that it was a time when the old educational categories for students suddenly came undone. Once educators began to take seriously the goal of providing an opportunity for every student to have access to an academic curriculum, they suddenly came face to face with all those kids who'd been ignored for so long. And so we gradually have taken on the serious responsibility of doing English with kids no longer like us. Sometimes this has meant crossing social-class boundaries; other times it has meant seeing new groups of immigrants, who began challenging us to extend the range of our multicultural and multilingual awareness.

Gordon: And boy was that scary because we weren't immediately equipped to work productively with all of these students, especially in urban areas . . .

John: . . . They simply didn't arrive at our classroom doors with the kind of cultural capital we used to expect. Plus they didn't have much patience for the traditional transmission of knowledge teaching that generations had put up with. Yet our profession hasn't exactly changed to meet these new imperatives, as I've extensively outlined in my book *Uncommon Sense* (Mayher, 1990). The tired old classroom routines work even less well with these new populations, except to keep them in their place, busy with worksheets and grammar drills. Still, the challenge of these "new" students hasn't exactly resulted in teachers as a group becoming aggressive in pursuing the many good ideas that build on what kids bring with them to the school.

Gordon: Of course, a lot of education talk has always centered around preparation for the workplace, and so the "commonsense" education that you have been railing against for years, John, is often about keeping students quiet. Except for the workers hired to "think," employers are pretty clear about wanting people who are punctual and follow directions. It should come as no surprise that much of the actual work required of workers will best be carried out in a state of compliance, because what they have to do is often mindless and repetitive.

John: Yes, and then when they speak out trying to expose an error or improve the system, like many whistle blowers, despite the rhetoric, they become pariahs, not heroes. This docility has to begin somewhere and generally it's in the school . . .

Gordon: Hey, who wants a student in class who is always challenging what we say? Who wants reason impinging on our own prerogatives? It can be dangerous when too many students move beyond repetitive motions and calculations and begin thinking about the big picture.

John: Students may even propose cutting through the red tape that sustains us and that we think is indispensable to our role as teachers, and whoa . . . our carefully prepared lesson plans might require dramatic revision!

Gordon: So in part what I think interests us both here is actually living up to what we thought was involved in a liberal arts education: speaking up. Not just a few specially privileged students speaking up, but seeing the

consequences of personal and social decisions in terms of spreading social justice. Thus we applaud whenever we see English teachers helping
their students gain some critical perspective on what humanity has so far
created and experienced and how far we still have to go.

John: It's hard to accept the extent to which tradition and power quietly determine the current way of doing things. Yes, don't upset the scripts
already in place. But we're also dealing with a psychological dimension
here. Remember, people resist change and psychologically find it difficult to entertain the prolonged uncertainty and exposure of incompe-
tence that come with the taking up or learning of new procedures . . .

Gordon: . . . which in turn involve perhaps new ways of relating to students.

John: Yet when we think critically with students, we often begin in a double-
bind situation, which has to make us skeptical of the motives behind the
enterprise. The first move is always easy. We recognize the value of sub-
jecting the behaviors and beliefs *of others* to scrutiny. The reciprocal second move is less so. Will it be worthwhile interrogating our own beliefs,
or the whole worldview supporting the institution that writes our checks
in the first place? So even those of us who lament the schools' inability to
create critical thinkers, or who worry about the dumbed-down curriculum fueled by mindless examinations, will be discovered to have our
blind side. There will be issues we might just take off the table in order to
keep peace in the ranks.

Gordon: So we're left with making distinctions. It's one thing trying to solve
the immediate problem of why a particular group of students is not doing
the reading or, worse, not even attending school—we can bring in rap
music or venture into their community and talk to their parents. Yet it's
quite another thing to question the entire social system that has created
the "nonlearning" conditions in the first place whereby certain students
lack the social and cultural capital to succeed in school. I know, we don't
want to just be taking some moral high road here. Despite our reform vision and efforts, the machinery hums along. So where does one pressure
for change when one senses an outrage has occurred? I am reminded of
the seeming futility when in late 2000 the Black Caucus in Congress
raised objections to the certification of Bush as president because of voting irregularities in Florida—they were ruled out of order.

John: Still, they were morally compelled to speak up, even if the system
would not take them seriously. And in fact they were expressing the first
rule of critical thinking: discrepancy detection. I suppose it's our fate inevitably to be surrounded by contradictions. Surely life and death, or our
sense of mortality in the midst of life, presents the fundamental contradiction we have to deal with as humans, but equity and justice are key
values behind any critical thinking effort, especially as it is defined by the

Western Enlightenment project of progress—no final right answers, no final truth, and so a history of trying to include more folks in the conversation, while unmasking the indefensible reasons for privilege and hegemony. This larger critical project ought to drive what goes on in the English classroom, not one focused on a functional or instrumental literacy that is satisfied with students fitting in and eventually making profits for someone else. *Critical thinking* should equip students to expose error, fraud, and fakery . . .

Gordon: —maybe even question privilege or status—and in doing so foster in students an ability to imagine new solutions to age-old dilemmas. It's not clear to me, however, that educators have been willing to really be open to any sustained critical thinking that might in fact expose all sorts of social conventions that will not stand up to scrutiny, especially when there is some sense of equity and fairness involved.

John: You're touching on the delicate matter of who will be in control. The politics of literacy have become dramatically evident in the United States with the accession of "George the 2nd" to the presidency, but the connection of the right to phonics instruction certainly has deep roots, as Jim Moffett (1988) was shocked to discover. After his English series was blown out of the water in West Virginia in the early 1970s, Jim wondered why a technique of teaching beginning reading had become a dogma of conservative politicians. His answer would have pleased George Orwell: Simply put, parents can be really nervous when they suspect some aspect of schooling may be encouraging their children to challenge parental authority and, in turn, the sacred texts. People who want to control interpretations of words, to limit them to a literal reading, believe that a phonics-centered approach to reading can achieve that. Whatever the reason for their "mind-control" goal—fascism, advertising, strict constructionism, patriarchy, "strict father morality," or fundamentalism—keeping texts under control seems like an essential tool.

Gordon: But, John, texts do have a way of slipping out of control even for phonics-trained readers, so it's crucial to mention the added bonus of a total phonics approach—make reading so-o-o boring that only the elite few who get a critical approach to literacy will continue to read.

John: I guess we can't avoid it . . . as English teachers today we are simply much more aware of these numerous struggles over authority. If you are in power it seems that one good strategy is keeping everything secret; thus authority thinks it can be protected from its opposition by controlling the texts.

Gordon: And at the local level this translates into families becoming upset over any program that encourages students to ask questions, for the ultimate questions a student might ask will sooner or later involve the matter of religious faith. You can hear them now: "These are our children and we don't want outsiders messing with their minds. We'll raise them as we like, thank you very much." Matters of faith and control are enough to raise a tempest in all too many communities.

John: Remember it was Moffett who presciently went on to warn that the next potential area for conflict—censorship and mind-control—was coming once students began to write more and more about real topics and expressed their real opinions. As long as most school writing was some mindless following of form—what Ken McCroire called "Engfish" (1970) and Jasper Neel "anti-writing" (1988)—namely, five-paragraph themes written formulaically on either side of a tired and essentially meaningless subject to the writer, then even if it stated a controversial position, no one need take it seriously. But once the formulas crack and student voices begin to be heard on issues that do matter to them, then immediately the iron hand of censorship is ready to shut down student newspapers, forbid the posting of compositions on bulletin boards, and reestablish control of what will be acceptable subjects for writing. High-stakes testing will of course get everyone back into step.

Gordon: Well, I knew we'd eventually get around to that. Testing, testing everywhere, it seems, but not a thought to think. Sadly, the major counterforce controlling student writing and thinking has not been overt censorship. Instead, it's fair to say that the major source of mindlessness we face today in education is the institution of more and more rigorous state testing programs in response to the call for higher educational standards. Such tests have a kind of preventive censoring effect when it comes to the development of literacy.

John: Well, what are we to expect? When instruction begins by focusing once again on the formal features of writing—spelling counts and so does grammar—and on the logical structures of prose, having an actual intention to say something worthwhile is easily neglected.

Gordon: Too messy, too out of control.

John: Not that there's anything wrong with either form or logic, of course, but when they are taught as the empty vessels of structure to be filled by whatever argument the test prompt demands, they risk becoming ideological straitjackets, not "enabling constraints." It is so much easier for teachers and students—and test evaluators—to focus on the skeletons of the prose they are writing and reading than on the meat, that the substance and essential driving force behind real writing gets short shrift.

Gordon: And, once again, the emphasis on form and standards brings back pressures to conform to a single linguistic standard. How ironic or predictable that at a time when more and more immigrants and more and more poor people are elbowing their way into higher education that the pressures on them to conform to "Standard Written English" are greater than ever. Grammar—that many-headed Hydra slain repeatedly by a century of research—is back with a vengeance in schools.

John: Indeed! Even otherwise quite progressive English teachers in training are willing once again to shoulder the burdens of the language police. We do so for benign reasons, of course, in our effort to make the playing field more level for those who were raised outside the linguistic mainstream. And we recognize that the pressures of the high-stakes tests that will determine promotion and graduation in many if not all of the soon to be *Unitized* States demand such linguistic conformity. Teaching prescriptive grammar, however, is not likely to work now any better than it ever has to accomplish these homogenizing ends. How can we get our colleagues to see that it is in fact doubly ineffective since it not only fails to deliver on its promise of help, but actually hurts children's chances of achieving writing and reading competence because it's robbing curricular time from real writing and reading experiences?

Gordon: I suppose one could argue that the high-stakes testing movement can serve a good purpose to the extent that it shines a bright light on our failure to meet our educational responsibility to all those previously underserved students, especially those living in areas where resources are not equally distributed.

John: Great, put the pressure on, but what's happened? In all too many cases the tests have retarded the kind of progressive practices that held great promise of reaching this new population we've been talking about. Of course, it also plays havoc with the kids that we most identify with. Isn't it sad how the system of confused standards creates false expectations in those who can least afford it? These pressures to conform create even more dramatic conflicts between nonmainstream children and the schools. Unfortunately, many parents and kids are willing to go along with the schools' demands because they have bought into the promise that education constitutes the path to material success.

Gordon: Still, many are not buying it, but mostly they are powerless, voiceless. And whether or not this previously underserved population agrees with the tyranny of testing and correct linguistic forms, the anger that they often feel at having to deny or reject their heritage pervades the stories of even those who are "winners." The words of Richard Rodriguez (1982), Keith Gilyard (1991), Patrick Chamoiseau (1997), Eva Hoffman (1989), and Maxine Hong Kingston (1989), to name a few, certainly give us a perspective different from the Establishment's party line. Their resentments are clear about the failure of the system to recognize their home identities.

John: And for the losers, the situation is even worse as their alienation grows.

The inspiration behind our system of democratic education was never to provide a sorting system for winners and losers, but to broaden access and mastery for all, a thing recognized in a seminal text in our field that still bears reading, *Growth Through English* (Dixon, 1967).

Gordon: John Dixon would certainly not be happy with how his concern for maturity and imagination, as it develops out of a quest for personal meaning, has been swept aside, all in the interests of keeping the global economy supercharged. You and I are hardly against standards. We even like to imagine ourselves as world class! But the words ring hollow. First, the standards game is generally played by emphasizing "output" standards, while ignoring "input" standards.

John: Yes, so it's easy to stand tall and demand that all students read and write at a particular competence level, but then fail to give the schools what they need to support these demands, whether it be smaller classes or adequate and rich reading materials.

Gordon: Right. On the surface who could be against "success for all" or "no child left behind"—as they called that act passed in 2001 under the "leadership" of the second Bush administration—but turn your back and the instructional funding has mysteriously failed to keep pace with the teaching requirements.

John: I'd say that's a blatant case of the "financial success" carrot leading the standards movement. I think you'd agree, however, that, worse than empty rhetoric, these are actually clever strategies for deflecting the public's awareness away from how underresourced our schools and teachers actually continue to be. Why do our public spaces have to end up being less important than private tax reductions? So unlike the halcyon days when we started out in this profession, we now are aware of how deeply political English is, because the kind of language use and inquiry that we seek to encourage and honor is always deeply social as it goes about supporting a sense of agency on the part of all students. And displaying such agency will surely step on many toes!

Gordon: Well, the American experiment keeps exposing these kinds of contradictions. The 1960s stirred up our awareness of social justice issues, which in turn meant acknowledging the fact that so many kids, despite our claims about universal secondary education (let alone integration), were not getting the education they were supposedly entitled to. The lack of resources are of course an important part of the problem, but as you've said many times, we simply haven't spent the necessary energy reconceptualizing ourselves as a field of study. We need to take into consideration much more than we do presently the radical social and economic shifts that characterize the environments within which we use language to make and interrogate meaning. And we have to admit that there are aesthetic shifts that we are no doubt not keeping up with—areas where, unless we can humbly be open to our own students being the teachers, our arrogance threatens to leave us clueless.

John: I see what you mean. Those kids who are different from us and then even the kids supposed to be like us have actually helped change the cultural environment that is part of what we study in English. The old distinctions between high and low culture may hold in the rarified halls of academe, but kids could care less. With the expansion of pop culture and the egalitarian values often found there, we have to rethink what kinds of materials are appropriate to bring into the classroom.

Gordon: And this presents a creative stimulus for mixing novelty with tradition because often you can't get the whole picture of what a writer or artist is trying to accomplish if you don't know the context and the possible antecedents provoking the text and the experiences it is committed to exploring.

John: So we have new kids with a new background as learners, we have our social justice mission, and we have a whole new range of possible texts that we might consider with them. We've had the adolescent literature movement, of course, which recognized a better match between text and the developmental level of the reader, but we have to do much more in sensing out the reading and writing profiles and interests of our students. I was reading an Australian study recently that reported that ninth-grade girls overwhelming prefer horror novels—now where do they get to read them in our curriculum?

Gordon: Not in too many classrooms that I'm aware of and even fewer as test preparation squeezes out the last drop of unaccounted-for time.

John: And beyond a world of "low-culture" texts and happenings, it's time to seriously contend with a technology and communication environment that we don't have a clue about if we go back to what we had to work with 40 years ago. I remember thinking how lucky we were to have written our dissertations when we had access to a Xerox machine and one of those IBM selectric typewriters with the speeding type ball. I couldn't imagine doing all this and only having carbon paper to make copies—but then, remember the days when we learned to do math calculations on a slide rule!

Gordon: Ah, the slide rule—now that was something I was good at! At least it alerted you to the creative aspect of estimation. It was more useful, it turned out, to understand a ballpark figure than to not know what was behind an exact number that some hand calculator spit out.

John: That's interesting. Precision is not always what it's cracked up to be. In fact, the seduction of a perfect surface can often cover up cracks deep beneath . . . But, as I was saying, moving from photography to cinema to television to personal computers and then to the Internet, each shift has not only made much more information available, it has also dramatically changed the ways we can express and analyze and present our ideas and thus our identities. With the printed word no longer the coin of the realm and thus the defining medium of English teachers, we're going to have to reimagine what actual communication skills we're teaching. Images of all sorts abound, but beyond this, English teachers need to come to terms with the very real tension between the linear organization of material that we've been used to and the new simultaneity of information that we must handle successfully if we are to survive with any semblance of sanity in today's multimedia world.

Gordon: Take hypertext for instance. It probably more closely represents how our minds process ideas and their associated referents, but the five-paragraph theme still dominates the landscape of writing instruction. If composing is now more about how concepts and information are endlessly linked and intertwined, then we have a major shift in what our responsibilities are when we engage in reading and writing with our students. Text production in this age of cyberspace means catching a reader/viewer's attention in new ways. If you can catch their attention long enough, then the logic of argument may also have to enter new territory.

John: It can be exhausting just thinking about keeping up with all these endless reversals of our expectations, being exposed to worlds and meanings we can no longer comfortably reproduce. But I suppose the very forms of our expression, what we're comfortable with, will continue to evolve.

Gordon: You have to laugh. . . . Several years ago, we wouldn't have imagined typing back and forth in a chat room to produce a chapter for this book, and thereby hopefully invite possibility, rather than assert closure.

John: So we're back to our own square one, which is even prior to English education. I'm thinking of what it means to do native language instruction. And this itself already comes filled with numerous problems when students don't even come equipped with *the* "native language." How are we going to mediate all these new constraints? How are we going to see them as opportunities for actually allowing our practices in the classroom to catch up with all those pedagogical theories over the years that have acknowledged the central role in education of the student's intentions, background, and ongoing experiences? For what we are about finally as English teachers is finding ways to help students become powerful language users, but the medium, and context within which this is happening, matter greatly. Thus we have to pay careful attention to exactly what we are collectively using English to create and investigate in the classroom.

Gordon: So, interestingly enough, with all this external change the kinds of values we've been advocating all along continue to be relevant. In taking all kids seriously, the "transactional approach" to reading literature becomes even more relevant. Similarly, working with all students is best served with a constructivist approach, one that fosters a student's agency and ownership. And when we talk about communication, process and product can't be separated. Multiple forms must be honored, for what we're doing as teachers is constantly revising, that is if we stand a chance of keeping up with our students.

John: Of course, none of this is going to be easy. But looking backward has value, if it can shed light on the present and, particularly, the future. All teaching should be future-oriented, of course, since our students will use whatever they learn with and from us throughout their lives long after they've forgotten us. But teaching teachers is doubly future-oriented, since the final effect reaches a second generation, the pupils of our students who won't even know we exist. Indeed, one of the reasons it is hard to assess the effectiveness of teacher education is that although the real payoff occurs in that second generation, there are so many intervening variables that the effect of a teacher's teacher education on her pupils is extraordinarily difficult to trace. Yet despite the empirical difficulties of tracking such effects, those of us who do teacher education remain convinced of its importance and its effectiveness, and we are equally sure it is crucial to any effort to reform or improve the learning lives of children and adolescents in school.

Gordon: That's right, many of us left K–12 classrooms reluctantly because we were convinced that we could multiply our teaching effectiveness by becoming teacher educators, and we've watched the careers of enough of our students to know that we are having those long-term effects.

John: We also know that teacher education never stops, because teacher learning never stops. Earning a teaching certificate may give you the right to enter a classroom, but your learning how to teach has just begun.

Gordon: And all veteran teachers know that they have had to keep learning in order to survive. We have to keep learning because the demands of the classroom keep changing; we have to keep learning because the culture keeps changing; we have to keep learning because the students keep changing; and we have to keep learning because the more we know, the more we understand how much more we need to learn.

John: And one of the benefits of this need for never-ending learning (Mayher

& Brause, 1991) is that it steadily reinforces the challenging excitement of teaching. Neither of us can imagine having been taught to do a job in our early twenties, having mastered it by our mid-twenties, and then still doing it 35 years later. What a boring prospect! So even with the difficulties, tensions, and frustrations of teaching, the opportunity for growth and change makes it continually renewing for those who have learned how to turn the challenges into opportunities.

Gordon: Thus wouldn't we agree that one of the basic realities of teacher education is how to maintain multiple angles of vision over time? We want to keep one focus on the prospective teacher's current learning in classrooms and in the field, another focus on the learning of the beginning teacher's present and future pupils, and still another focus on the teacher as learner so that when they do leave us to enter their own classroom they will have a capacity to keep on learning and growing throughout their careers.

John: I just wish we could get the public to realize how complex and stressful teaching is. Certainly, without the resilience and reflectivity of being lifelong learners, no teacher can survive the pressures and anxieties of the job. To prepare for that, future teachers need both the practical experiences and hands-on tips they desperately crave and a broad and deep theoretical framework, which they often resist as impractical and therefore useless.

Gordon: So we want this book to speak to both beginning and experienced teachers, and we hope it will contribute to their ongoing growth in a number of aspects: There are some practical looks at how to enhance teacher-student transactions in contemporary secondary classrooms, and there are provocative challenges to the conceptual status quo that most of us have brought to teaching.

John: Further, we want to promote the kind of reframing of the problems of teaching and learning in English that will be essential if substantive change is to occur. One of the ongoing challenges of teaching in both theory and practice is how to free ourselves from a slavish dependence on our own school experience as the primary determinant of how we teach. The "educational common sense" that all of us acquired during our 12,000-plus hours of school experience runs deep in our unconscious definitions of the norms of practice, and until it is recognized and challenged, no "uncommon sense" conceptions and practices can flourish. But my typing fingers are getting tired, so over and out for now.

Gordon: Okay, John, but at least thanks to this new medium our 35-year conversation has begun yet again.

[John logs out.]
[Gordon logs out.]

REFERENCES

Chamoiseau, P. (1997). *School days*. Lincoln: University of Nebraska Press.

Commission on English. (1965). *Freedom and discipline in the teaching of English*. New York: College Entrance Examination Board.

Dixon, J. (1967). *Growth through English: A report based on the Dartmouth seminar, 1966*. Oxford: Oxford University Press for the National Association for the Teaching of English.

Gilyard, K. (1991). *Voices of the self: A study of language competence*. Detroit, MI: Wayne State University.

Hoffman, E. (1989). *Lost in translation*. New York: Dutton/Plume.

Kingston, M. H. (1989). *Woman warrior: Memoir of a girlhood among ghosts*. New York: Random House.

Mayher, J. (1990). *Uncommon sense: Theoretical practice in language education*. Portsmouth, NH: Boynton/Cook.

Mayher, J., & Brause, R. (Eds.) (1991). *Search and re-search: What the inquiring teacher needs to know*. New York: Taylor & Francis.

McCroire, K. (1970). *Uptaught*. Rochelle Park, NJ: Hayden.

Moffett, J. (1988). *Storm in the mountains: A case study of censorship, conflict, and consciousness*. Carbondale: Southern Illinois University Press.

Neel, J. (1988). *Plato, Derrida, and writing*. Carbondale: Southern Illinois University Press.

Pradl, G. (1996). *Literature for democracy: Reading as a social act*. Portsmouth, NH: Boynton/Cook.

Rodriguez, R. (1982). *Hunger of memory: The education of Richard Rodriguez*. New York: Bantam, Doubleday, Dell.

Rosenblatt, L. (1995). *Literature as Exploration* (5th ed.). New York: Modern Language Association. (Original edition published 1938)

CHAPTER 2

A History Not Yet Past: Where Then Is Here?

JOHN WILLINSKY
University of British Columbia

My contribution to this book addresses contemporary issues in Canadian secondary English studies; as luck would have it, there is nothing either strictly contemporary or entirely Canadian about these issues. But that is the way with such issues. They are nothing without understanding their broader context. It is my duty and pleasure to provide something of a historical context for the issues that follow, in the belief that even a brief acquaintance with this history can open the door that much wider on what we, as English teachers, have the opportunity of doing with our classes and the world. My conviction is that to walk into an English class is to step onto a historical stage, even when there are no pictures of William Shakespeare or Matthew Arnold on the wall, and even if you are unaware of that history.

You might compare this to something as simple as speaking English. The language's history is embedded in the very sound, structure, and spelling of the words, even though you can go on speaking well enough while being unaware of that history. But having an interest in that history is something of what it means to be a teacher of English, something of what it means to participate in both the traditions and the future of this passion for the language and its literature.

Teachers of English education and language arts work within the flow of a particular history, a history which they carry forward at some points, see changing at others, and themselves change at still others. Nowhere is that historical sense more apparent than among the many English teachers in Canada working with increasing numbers of students whose native tongue is other than English. This poses new challenges and opportunities for teachers in this postcolonial era, while at the same time connecting them to the very origins of their profession in earlier colonial times. Whether we are considering the multicultural qualities of the reading we are assigning or how to encourage students to write out the story of their own lives, we are invoking the history of English teaching, a history that is not yet past. To catch sight of this history is to begin working more effectively and more knowingly with and against those traditions.

Now, you may be thinking that whatever this history, English teaching really rides on the wings of the teachers' passion for literature and language. And while such passion does carry a class far and wide, we should not kid ourselves about how the job is also framed and funded by the political and cultural aspirations of provincial schooling systems. The thrill unfailingly felt by a teacher on reading from *Romeo and Juliet* is bound to be tempered by what needs to be covered and corrected snapping at her heels. This history, too, may just seem to get in the way of engaging with the timeless poetry, interfering with what drew us into the trade. Against that belief, I am here to redeem the educational value to be found in attending to that history and politics.

The connection between the passion and the history is captured, for me, in the historical struggle for self-expression and self-determination among people, for that area is where literature and language intersect with basic human rights and democratic action. This assertive articulation can be in the brave, convention-defying name of love, or it can be in the name of the many languages in the community. Although English teaching has sometimes been on the wrong side of the struggle for self-determination, it can help students experience and gain insight into those rights and powers, and do so in ways that can reshape the history of English teaching. This seems to me reason enough to open a book such as this with three broad moments from this history, beginning with those early postcolonial days of nineteenth-century Canada, through the educational progressivism of the early twentieth century, to the postwar rise of Canadian literary nationalism, feminist criticism, and multiculturalism.

COLONIAL ORIGINS

Although it can sometimes seem to English teachers that their subject has always, and has rightly, been at the center of the school timetable, the first important historical lesson here is that "English" doesn't go back that far compared to other subjects, nor are its origins even English in the sense of having its origins in the classrooms of England. The story of English teaching begins in nineteenth-century India. One can roughly date the launch of English literature as a distinct school subject to the passing of the 1835 English Education Act in India.[1] The English Education Act made English the language of instruction in the Indian schools under British colonial control. The Act was inspired by the recommendations of the historian Thomas Macaulay, whose famous 1835 Minute to the British government on what should be done about colonial education pointed out that, in his estimation, the whole of Indian literature was unworthy of a shelf of English writing. The teaching of English was a benevolent action intended to create an appreciation among the Indian people for what humanity could achieve in its highest form. English was intended to offer Indian students much the same opportunity to know greatness that Latin served for British students in the public schools of Britain.

Nearly 2 decades later, in 1853, the Orientalist Horace Wilson was able to advise the British Parliament that, as "we initiate [the Indians] into our literature, particularly at an early age, and get them to adopt feelings and sentiments from our standard writers, we make an impression upon them, and affect considerable alteration in their feelings and notions" (quoted by Viswanathan, 1989, p. 48). Literature teaching was thought capable of shaping a people's character. As it reflected the genius of a people, so it would not only serve as a model of civilized being to others, but would work upon them in the colonial schools as a "mask of conquest," in Gauri Viswanathan's phrase.[2]

What proved fit for the improvement of native children in colonial schools was then thought suitable for the industrial classes of Great Britain. Among English literature's great educational advocates at the time was Matthew Arnold. This is not Arnold as poet but as charity-school inspector. He was among the first to champion the subliminal usefulness of English poetry for the education of the disadvantaged: "Good poetry does," he advocated in his 1880 inspector's report to the Privy Council, "undoubtedly tend to form the soul and character" (Arnold, 1908, p. 60). And so the anthology of literature's "greatest hits," calibrated for different ages, became a mainstay of the English classroom. On the other hand, English literature had a decidedly more difficult time finding a home as a discrete academic discipline in the great universities of Oxford and Cambridge, where it presumably was not needed to shape soul and character and where the classics served as the basis of a literary education (Palmer, 1965).

During this period Canada had entered its own postcolonial state of nationhood and was the site of much educational activity on behalf of English literature. Judging from the evidence amassed by the distinguished scholar Bob Morgan, English literature had a large role to play in the country's smooth transition from colony to dominion. This evidence ranges from the composition topics assigned at University College in Toronto—where students had to write on the topic, "The connection between literary excellence and natural greatness, as exhibited in English history"—to the declarations of educator Henry Scalding that Shakespeare was "virtually a type of colonist . . . appreciated among the junior members of the family of nations—among the human downrootings from the great mothertree of England" (Morgan, 1990, pp. 209, 213). In advance of Matthew Arnold, George Paxton Young, architect of

English studies in Ontario, advised in his Department of Education Report for 1867–68 that *The Merchant of Venice* "was a lesson in practical Christian Ethics . . . [that] can scarcely be read intelligently without entering into the soul and becoming part of its convictions for ever" (quoted in Morgan, 1990, p. 203).[3]

Young's conviction should be enough to give one pause over the continuing place of *The Merchant of Venice* in the high school curriculum and exemplifies how the unquestionable literary greatness of a work was readily directed at what today, at least, we would see as the extraliterary purposes of schooling the young. This sense of literature's educational mission was built on the language of spiritual salvation. From India to Canada, no less than at home in Great Britain, students were to be infused with this civilizing testament to the mother country's natural moral and literary greatness. And while we have long since secularized literature teaching, our tendency is still to focus on the ethical and moral dilemmas raised by literary works, which continues the civilizing mission at this teaching trade's origins.

Those wonderful class-stopping moments that grab hold of the quality of mercy or the ethics of conversion in *The Merchant of Venice* need not be given up. However, on those same questions, the class could also consider what it has meant for Canadian schools to teach this play to generations of young Christian and non-Christian students, without addressing, until recently, whether it might be presenting a prejudicial view of the Jewish people, at least judging from the questions posed in the back of earlier if not current school editions. We need to appreciate how our best intentions can still fall within or work against that historical faith in literature's unconscious powers.

This colonial legacy can also be found in the much-taught instance of William Golding's *Lord of the Flies*, which stands as a "children's" version of Conrad's *Heart of Darkness*.[4] The planeload of schoolboys stranded on that proverbial deserted island enact a similar and equally repulsive and fascinating reversion to the primitive state of native peoples. Again, there is the opportunity, if not the responsibility, to help students appreciate how such island and jungle fantasies work. They can see how such images evoke a sense of primitive lives that was once necessary to colonial ways of dividing the world between those who are civilized and those in need of civilizing (and rescuing and conversion in *Lord of the Flies* and *The Merchant of Venice*). Otherwise, recapitulating the original civilizing mission remains a real danger for the English classroom of today.

Now I would emphasize that this play on the divisions between people is but one structural feature of significance in these works, and to see how such ideas about the primitive and the civilized served people then and now is only one of many lessons that can be learned with these works. But to teach such lessons, while keeping in mind how teaching English literature was originally intended to civilize those who could at best only approximate young English-men, is to begin to challenge and change that history on both literary and ed-ucational fronts. This is not, then, about proscribing the teaching of any given piece of literature. It is about teaching students how a work of literature, as a force in the world, can be used for many purposes, including, at times, to jus-tify the conquering spirit of an imperial power. To introduce this history is to expand the students' critical skills so that it encompasses the scope and purpose of their own education as something that will need to be revised as ours has had to be. It is about helping the young determine literature's and education's place in their lives, and this would be to take English in decidedly progressive direc-tions.

PROGRESSIVE DIRECTIONS

During this century, the most radical of challenges to education's civilizing urge came from the progressive education movement. As the name suggests, progressive educators were more interested in the world that lay ahead than in looking back to the cultural legacy that students needed to absorb. It was about embracing the prospects of progress, the progress of democracy and science in urban and industrial societies, with the American philosopher John Dewey (1916) and the Italian educator Maria Montessori (1909/1964) among its best-known sources of inspiration. Dewey, for example, insisted that the center of the curriculum was not the great works of a culture, but the very experience of the child. It is that crediting of the child's own experience that connects this movement to democratic concerns.

In English teaching, these efforts to bring the student's experience to the fore were best realized in the groundbreaking work of Louise Rosenblatt. She taught at New York University for many years and has been no small influence on Canadian English teaching (in ways comparable to the later influence of British progressive initiatives associated with James Britton and language for learning). For example, the provincial guides in language arts of a few years ago, when I was teaching in Alberta, liberally drew on Rosenblatt in spirit and language to shape their approach to reading and literature (Alberta Education, 1987).

The roots of her influence go back to the early decades of this century. Im-migration and new industrial technologies were beginning to transform this continent into far more of an urban mass society. For its part, progressive edu-cation sought to foster the value and experience of each individual, with edu-cation providing the resources for participating in the greater good. In a theme that runs through other chapters in this book, Louise Rosenblatt shifted the fo-cus of English teaching from exposing students to the meaning of great works to developing the students' own experiences with, and responses to, literature. It is important to note that this was not simply a motivational trick directed at attracting students' attention. This recognition of the individual's experience and expression was inspired by a political commitment to expanding democratic participation in this culture. Each reader counts. Each student's experience is worth nurturing, facilitating, and encouraging.

Rosenblatt was to write her landmark of progressive literary education, *Literature as Exploration*, under the auspices of the Progressive Education Association's Commission on Human Relations in 1938. It was the heyday of progressivism, and Rosenblatt's pragmatic vision of progressive literary education was set to equip the young "with tools and the knowledge necessary for a scientifically objective, critical appraisal of accepted opinion" as well as providing the basis of "working out a more fruitful living" (Rosenblatt, 1938, p. 212). She also pointed to the vicarious experience afforded by literature, which could improve what were then known as "race relations." Her later work focused on how readers "live through" what she called "the reading event," with an emphasis on their aesthetic experience (Rosenblatt, 1978, p. 22). Her focus on the reader's engagement with the artfulness of literature was helpful both in personalizing the act of literary criticism and in distinguishing English teaching from social studies (think of how *To Kill a Mockingbird* is used to teach about racism). Yet it also tended to move away from those original concerns by equipping students with the critical skills to join in the dialogue over fruitful living.[5]

Today, then, we need to pause over this progressive legacy. We need to ask why we place this emphasis on students developing their own voice as readers and writers. Progressive education did not see the development of that voice as an end in itself. The goal was not a room full of children shouting to the rooftops in clear, articulate, and idiosyncratic voices about their favorite reading. The progress at issue here was originally about engagement and articulation as a basis of exchange; it was about challenging and testing ideas as a basis for collaboration and community; it was about literature as a meeting of public and private space within mass society, where the constant challenge is still finding, in the face of differences, a common basis for democratic action.

The progressive tradition is still with us today, not only in reader-response criticism, but in whole language, language across the curriculum, and life-writing, in learning to read those representations, see how texts are worked, and contribute to them as ways in which individuals and communities, corporate bodies and governments, write the world. The force of language is at issue here, and the English teacher is, in this progressive sense, engaged in teaching students about the subtle and blunt sides to this force.

What keeps this approach within the democratic hopes of progressive education is that this coming together, this articulation of experience and response, enables a greater degree of self-determination and public participation for more people. It is not enough, then, to regard the progressive movement as having moved the classroom beyond the teacher dictating the meaning and significance of the assigned novel, the symbols and metaphors of note in the poem before them. Students need to learn to trust and articulate their sense of the text and the world, seeing how texts shape worlds. They need, as Dewey put it, "a large variety of shared undertakings and experiences" (Dewey, 1916, p. 84). They need to become better students of how people respond to and understand the world through texts and screens. They need to consider how to work with people in making something more of that world, something more against the force of our biases and ways of dividing the world, something more in a sense that we can comfortably call *progress.*[6]

One of the striking and handy lessons on how the world can be contained, and our responses to it constrained, by certain texts is found in the changing syllabus of the literature class. When it comes to helping a class feel the force of this history, to taking its artifacts in hand, I have been recommending that teachers lead students down to the school bookroom. In most schools, the bookroom holds a terrific archive of older texts, each set of which carries within it the shape of this history, the course of this progress. A scanning of the authors and titles, the anthologies' tables of contents, the prefaces and questions in the back, will reveal a slow expansion of who counts as an author and what counts as literature, as education, as Canadian—which brings me to a third historical moment indispensable for understanding contemporary issues in Canadian secondary English studies.

CANLIT, GENDERED, AND MULTICULTURAL IDENTITIES

After the Second World War, when independence and nationalist movements were succeeding in finally bringing an end to the crumbling colonial empires of Europe, Canada was to feel its own belated postcolonial determinations in an upsurge of nationalism. The country sought to assert its cultural independence as a nation, or more accurately as a series of nations within a nation-state, with the "quiet revolution" in Quebec and sovereignty claims of the First Nations peoples, while the search in English Canada for that overarching national identity often took a literary turn.

In the late 1950s, Malcolm Ross started to edit the New Canadian Library (NCL), which was intended as a declaration of literary independence for English-language culture, beginning with Frederick Philip Grove's *Over Prairie Trails.* "Our literature was coming of age," Hugo McPherson noted in his introduction to Gabrielle Roy's *The Tin Flute*, fifth in the NCL series, playing on Roy's recognition in America and France (McPherson, 1969, p. v). The New Canadian Library was eventually to reach back to the "confederation poets"

(Charles G. D. Roberts, Bliss Carmen, Archibald Lampman, and Duncan Campbell Scott) in its efforts to re-create a national literature that began with the birth of the nation.[7]

For many of us, the New Canadian Library (initially printed and bound in Aylesbury, Bucks, England) was a badge of literary patriotism. Although many held that this national literature only served to reflect the differences among the regions that made up this land, it was enough for a writer of material suitable for school or college to be born or to have written within the borders of Canada to be taught and studied under the rubric of "CanLit." The common idea was that "teaching Canadian literature," as two Alberta educators, Robert Cameron and John Oster (1992) claimed, "allows students to see themselves through literature and, therefore, helps develop a sense of identity" (p. 21). Ah, that rub again, with English teachers pushing the sheer idiosyncratic individuality of literature's gifts against these singular senses of national literature and identity.

Sure, it says something about a nation to place authors like Margaret Laurence, despite the bannings, and Margaret Atwood on its prescribed list of Canadian authors.[8] But what "sense of identity" did one develop if these Canadian writers were obviously not writing about you? Did that make you a non-Canadian of nonidentity? CanLit was intended to push us beyond colonial ties to England and preserve us from the creeping continentalism from the south.[9] But it posed another sort of danger since this nationalism became identified with a culture, as if literature written by people living in this land was not proof enough that talk of a national character and identity represented, at its least damaging, a failure of perception and imagination.

Although English teachers may well be tempted to claim the cultural center of the national educational experience, taking responsibility for forming future Canadians through Canadian literature, there is another way. I am drawn, for example, to how this country's supercritic and English teachers' English teacher, Northrop Frye (1971), proposed that the identity question is really, "Where is here?" (p. 220).[10] This makes of every poem and story a mapping of what has been made of *here*. It is to ask us, as I would interpret the question, to gather our classes around this project of how *here* has been written, who has been written out of that definition, and how we are now to write it. It is to ask how, by this novel, that poem, and these questions, are we answering the question, answering it in ways that reflect an understanding of the educational history of such answers, in our continuing reading of *The Merchant of Venice* perchance, and in the continual rewriting of those earlier answers through Mordecai Richler's *Duddy Kravitz* and Joy Kogawa's *Obasan* and on, one hopes, to the works of Lee Maracle and Dionne Brand.

This leads into two further dimensions of this identity and literature question. The global assertion of human rights and equality in the postwar period also found expression in the feminist movement which was to have a major impact on the complete spectrum of human activity, including literary criticism. In Canadian English classes this took many forms, often entailing a shift in the focus of attention from the male heroics of character and author to the overlooked and other, whether in *Romeo and Juliet* or Atwood's early poetry.[11] The English classroom could now become a place to challenge having to learn to read like a man. It was a place to challenge what it meant to find oneself written by gender and genre, and what it meant to write for oneself against those images, including those of the great literary critics.[12] This was to take reader response another step along. It caught hold of how the teaching of English is about what is so thoroughly personal and what is so clearly held in common across categories of experience such as gender. It is to have students read within and against the history of that category.

This interest in human rights also made it apparent that this country's history of racially restrictive immigration and voting rights was a democratically inappropriate response to its cultural diversity. Canada did adopt multiculturalism as a national policy in 1971, and passed the Canadian Multiculturalism Act in 1987. The legislation was intended to ensure that people have the "freedom . . . to preserve, enhance, and share [their] cultural heritages" (*Multiculturalism*, 1987, p. 18). Although much has been said about the ensuing debate around multicultural and antiracist approaches in education, it should be noted that the cultural rights identified in the act have much to do with an English class getting at "where is here."[13]

The act could be interpreted, for example, as encouraging English teachers and students to look for ways of helping people in their community to realize their legal rights by preserving, enhancing, and sharing their cultural heritages, and to do so through the multilingual forms necessary for that. After all, who else in the community is as concerned with learning about the power and variety of language? This form of *service learning*, as it is sometimes called, could well teach lessons to students and community about how answering the question of "where is here" changes through acts of reading and writing. The resulting anthologies, narratives, reviews, translations, readings, and even technical documents and marketing materials would return us to the opening theme of how the contemporary issues that English teachers face today need to be seen within a context in which the past is still with us.

In the chapters that follow in this book, I invite you to consider how the contemporary issues that English teachers face grow out of these origins and legacies. Whether in thinking about new arts of reading, learner-centered assessments, or using the Internet to reach a larger world, we have the obligation and opportunity of finding our bearings, of setting the direction with a class, in relation to the history that otherwise carries us along. Each class we spend teaching the young about language's wonders, force, and power enacts a period's worth of traffic on this historical stage. And as for the impact of the lessons that follow on the course of that history in this book, "The which if you with patient ears attend, What here shall miss, our toil shall strive to mend" (Prologue, *Romeo and Juliet*).

NOTES

1. This section on colonial history draws on work in my *Learning to Divide the World* (pp. 219–223).

2. Viswanathan quotes the following from *Madras Christian Instructor and Missionary Record* from 1844: "The genius of literature . . . clearly sees . . . that she has found the men who are to extend her empire to the ends of the earth, and give her throne a stability that will be lasting as the sun" (Viswanathan, 1989, p. 166).

3. So it is, perhaps, that the play, as I noted earlier, was my high school introduction to Shakespeare in Grade 9, as it has proved to be for my youngest son.

4. Arthur Applebee's research on the "most popular titles of book length works, grades 9–12" ranks *Lord of the Flies* in tenth place in America for public schools (54 percent use it); it rises to third place at the Grade 12 level (Applebee, 1993, pp. 65, 68).

5. What it can do very well, as I've witnessed in Peter Prest's Calgary classroom, is set up "a dynamic atmosphere of trust, discussion, enthusiasm and acceptance in the classroom, one that approximates as closely as possible the true reader-text relationship" (Prest & Prest, 1988, p. 131).

6. Consider Dewey's statement: "And there is perhaps no better definition of culture than that it is the capacity for constantly expanding the range and accuracy of one's perception of meanings" (Dewey, 1916, p. 123).

7. Malcolm Ross had been somewhat apologetic over casting them as "confederation" poets, as owning that they were not "avowed and self-conscious prophets of the new Canadian nationalism" (Ross, 1960, p. ix).

8. When secondary students were asked in 1996 by the Writers in Electronic Residence program about their favorite Canadian authors, Kevin Major and Lucy Maud Montgomery were their first two choices, with Margaret Atwood third (http://www.edu.yorku.ca/~weir/weircanlit.html).

9. W. John Harker (1987), for example, writes of the importance of teaching Canadian literature "during a time when its national institutions and national character are being eroded by a kind of continentalism and internationalism based on political and economic expediency rather than on any sense of the long-term good of the country" (p. 425).

10. Frye offers an excellent example of how the "where is here" question gets answered in our trade. He managed to define *here* through a series of works on CanLit, some of which were collected in the diminutively entitled *The Bush Garden*, where *here* is encumbered by this primitiveness known as "the bush" and the unnamed peoples who

are identified with it, against which he and other English teachers have planted a garden in the form of what he called "world literature," namely Blake, the Bible, or Shakespeare. Frye demonstrated the power and privilege of defining *here* by the pattern of his reading and what he asked of his students.

11. On a feminist approach to the teaching of *Romeo and Juliet*, see Willinsky and Bedard (1989).

12. For the teaching of feminist writing among high school students, see Harper (1999), and for the feminist engagement with Frye, see Bogdan (1992).

13. The same year as the Multiculturalism Act (1987), the Ontario Ministry of Education published John Borovilos and Suwanda Sugunasiri's multicultural literature guideline, with Borovilos's anthology *Breaking Through* following not long after, in 1990. See Greenlaw (1996) on the multiculturalism and antiracism approaches to English teaching in the Ontario context and Bannerji (1993) for the feminist analysis of multiculturalism.

REFERENCES

Alberta Education. (1987). *Junior high languages curriculum guide*. Edmonton: Alberta Education.

Applebee, A. (1993). *Literature in the secondary school: Studies of curriculum and instruction in the United States*. Urbana, IL: National Council of Teachers of English.

Arnold, M. (1908). *Reports on elementary schools, 1852–1882*. London: HMSO.

Bannerji, H. (Ed.). (1993). *Returning the gaze: Essays on racism, feminism and politics*. Toronto: Sister Vision Press.

Bogdan, D. (1992). *Re-educating the imagination: Toward a poetics, politics, and pedagogy of literary engagement*. Upper Montclair, NJ: Boynton/Cook.

Borovilos, J., & Sugunasiri, S. (1987). *Multicultural literature within the English curriculum*. Toronto: Ontario Ministry of Education.

Borovilos, J. (1990). *Breaking through: A Canadian literary mosaic*. Scarborough, ON: Prentice-Hall.

Cameron, R., & Oster, J. (1992). The great Canadian literature debate. *Alberta English*, *30*(2), 21–26.

Cremin, L. A. (1961). *The transformation of the school: Progressivism in American education, 1876–1957*. New York: Knopf.

Dewey, J. (1916). *Democracy and education*. New York: Free Press.

Frye, N. (1971). *The bush garden: Essays on the Canadian imagination*. Toronto: Anansi.

Greenlaw, J. (1996). The evolution of antiracism in Ontario's high school English classrooms [Review of M. Ibrahim Allandin's *Racism in Canadian Schools*]. *Journal of Educational Administration and Foundations*, *11*(2), 70–85.

Harker, W. J. (1987). Canadian literature in Canadian schools: From the old to the new internationalism. *Canadian Journal of Education*, *12*(3), 417–427.

Harper, H. (1999). *Dangerous desires: High school girls and feminist writing practices*. New York: Peter Lang.

McPherson, H. (1969). Introduction. In G. Roy, *The tin flute* (pp. v–xi). Toronto: McClelland & Stewart.

Montessori, M. (1964). *The Montessori method* (A. E. George, Trans.). New York: Schocken Books. (Original work published 1909)

Morgan, R. (1990). The "Englishness" of English teaching. In I. Goodson & P. Medway (Eds.), *Bringing English to order* (pp. 197–241). London: Falmer Press.

Multiculturalism . . . being Canadian. (1987). Ottawa, ON: Ministry of Supply and Services.

Palmer, D. J. (1965). *The rise of English studies: An account of the study of English language and literature from its origins to the making of the Oxford English School.* London: Oxford University Press.

Prest, P., & Prest, J. (1988). Clarifying our intentions: Some thoughts on the application of Rosenblatt's transactional theory of reading in the classroom. *English Quarterly, 21*(2), 127–133.

Rosenblatt, L. (1938). *Literature as exploration.* For the Commission on Human Relations. New York: Appleton-Century.

Rosenblatt, L. (1978). *The reader, the text, the poem: The transactional theory of literature.* Carbondale: Southern Illinois University Press.

Ross, M. (1960). Introduction. In M. Ross (Ed.), *Poets of the Confederation* (pp. ix–xiv). Toronto: McClelland & Stewart.

Viswanathan, G. (1989). *Masks of conquest: Literary study and British rule in India.* New York: Columbia University Press.

Willinsky, J. (1998). *Learning to divide the world.* Minneapolis: University of Minnesota.

Willinsky, J., & Bedard, J. (1989). *The fearful passage: Romeo and Juliet in the high school: A feminist perspective.* Ottawa, ON: Canadian Council of Teachers of English.

CHAPTER 3

Uncertain Relations: English and Cultural Studies

ROBERT MORGAN
Ontario Institute for Studies in Education, University of Toronto

Cultural studies is a multidisciplinary movement that arose from the social sciences and humanities after midcentury and breaks new ground in critical approaches to culture by placing it "in the context of its social and political embeddedness" (Bennett, 1991, pp. 37–38). In practice this means exploring culture as individual texts, local signs and symbols, everyday practices, and felt experiences on the one hand, and simultaneously as institutionally grounded representations, shared "structures of feeling," systemic regimes of discourse, and historically sedimented practices on the other. It is never enough, however, to provide just one photograph of cultural studies. Definitions vary almost as widely as practitioners, who value its lack of fixity and continuous reconstruction in light of changing needs and circumstances. It has been described as both a disciplinary and a de-disciplinary formation, one asserting the paramount importance of cultural practices yet steadfastly refusing "to explain everything from the cultural point of view" (Grossberg, 1996, p. 180).

In order to convey a sense of what this approach has to say to English teachers, I start from the question, How does cultural studies define culture? At the end of the first section, I provide a summarizing definition of what Williams calls this "wooly monster." Next, I ask what is involved in "doing cultural studies" in terms of its methods of analysis. Finally, I turn to questions of practice for English teachers interested in drawing on this perspective. The chapter ends with a description of a project that I have personally found useful in imparting and grounding this approach in the classroom as well as some final suggestions about other work along these lines.

Behind my opening questions lurk still others, such as Gunter Kress's (1995) inquiry into what an English curriculum for the future might look like, one that facilitates a culture of innovation, difference, and exchange. Other backstage questions haunt those mentioned above: What does an ethical-political commitment to the concept of social literacy (versus functional literacy, media literacy, computer literacy, and so forth) now involve? How can social literacy concretely promote democratic relations not only in English classrooms but in everyday life? Another way to put this is to ask, What does it mean to teach English with an awareness of recent shifts in cultural theory, an increasingly mediatized social space, multicultural realities, and globalized interchanges? Do faculties of education yet register these seismic shifts in the ways they prepare English teachers? Or, more sharply I might ask, Do these institutions still train teachers for past cultural revolutions, print, oracy and literate values alone, and the "civilizing mission" that has defined English from its birth a century ago?

These are, of course, impossibly large questions and any answers below are merely suggestive rather than definitive of a cultural studies position, partly because of its refusal of any fixed method or totalizing explanations (cf. Grossberg, 1996, p. 179). Yet it is from just such questions that the impulse for cultural studies begins: from the pressing need to address the bad new media as well as good old literary texts, from modern communications technologies apprehended as new powers of speech, from commodity culture as well as canonic culture. If, as Raymond Williams (1975) states, "our way of seeing things is our way of living" and "the process of communication is in fact the process of community" (p. 38), then electronic media are now central to the dynamics of identity, otherness, social relations, knowledge, and power. My intention therefore is to clarify what is at stake in a cultural studies approach and to suggest that its theoretical framework troubles English teaching as we have known it. I also hope to illustrate that cultural studies is not just about critique and deconstruction, as commonly thought. It is equally about practice, "propelled by the desire to construct possibilities, both immediate and imaginary" (Grossberg, 1996, p. 179) out of local circumstances and lived problems. In this sense, within schools it is committed to developing curricula that deal with the shifting "boundaries of differentiation" (Kennedy, 1992, p. 41) encountered in the everyday signs, commodities, and cultural experiences of students.

A brief anecdote might help to illustrate what I mean about the link between technological change and the emergence of cultural studies. Marshall McLuhan once said that when a form of media becomes dominant, people stop paying attention to it. For English teachers, the reverse is typically the case. As official custodians of literacy and literature for more than a century, we have preserved and attended to voice and print in loving detail, helping to maintain them as dominant media forms. For example, in the late-nineteenth-century school, Readers and Reciters reinforced the message that "reading or writing well" led to mastery of the public modes of communication. Selections in such texts were chosen as much for their oratorical flourish, as for their suitability for special occasions, and literary merit. Prefaces often contained a section entitled "principles of elocution," with diagrams on the correct alignment of the body, sketches of appropriate facial expressions for particular effects, and directions on how to best organize public speech; and schools regularly awarded prizes for "perfect recitation" and public speaking. All this attention to public speech was consistent with the link between oracy and power in the 1800s, evident, for instance, in professions like law, the ministry, or government. Yet, at the very moment of the fullest flowering of elocutionary manuals in schools, oratorical skills were already being displaced. To put the case sharply, even before Alexander Melville Bell's texts *On Teaching Reading in Public Schools* (1879) and *Standard Elocutionist* (1882) were in use in schools, his son Alexander Graham Bell had already reproduced the sound of the human voice by electronic means. Information about this new medium was disseminated by newspapers that were receiving much of their information by telegraph. "Wireless radio" was developed over the next decade by Marconi, with the first transatlantic transmission in 1901. The "Bell curve" of my story, if you will, is that English teachers have continued to privilege voice and print long after other media forms have moved to the center of life and begun transforming the way we live and relate.

Cultural studies arises, then, as a way of trying to understand profound social, technological, material, and theoretical changes—how they shape our own historical moment and how we might address questions that traditional disciplinary formations often ignore. Again, I want to insist that what centrally defines cultural studies as a transdisciplinary project is not just that it asks novel questions and provides new conceptual resources for thinking about mutations in cultural technology, the politics of everyday life, or the changing shape of society. At a minimum it seeks to provide marginalized groups with "strategies for survival and resistance" (Hall, 1990a, p. 22); more proactively, it fosters ways of cutting into the real so as to facilitate more democratic, participatory relations.

Cultural studies also makes strong theoretical demands of its practitioners. One reason for this is that cultural theory provides a way of moving back and forth between the study of a specific cultural text and a larger set of discourses concerned "with the shape and texture of a whole culture" (Eagleton, 1991, p. 8). Another is that theory opens up what Homi Bhabha (1988) calls a "third space": a moment between living in culture and our traditional explanations of it (p. 10). At its best, theory is a "space of translation" where new questions, new expectations, and categories of understanding start to emerge, "a sign that history is happening . . . within the systems and structures we construct" to try to understand the world (p. 11). Practical teaching strategies thus arise for cultural studies pedagogy only after you wrestle with its theoretical framework and come to inhabit some of its concepts—especially since many of them challenge aspects of English.

The tensions between English and cultural studies have usefully been described by John Frow (1992) in terms of four crises of humanistic disciplines in the late twentieth century. First, there is a crisis of theoretical objects. No longer, for example, is the term *text* simply restricted to written works, but it is applied to music videos, clothing, social events, or shopping malls, to name just a few of its current extensions. Nor do terms like *intertextuality* stop its unraveling since, applied to social practices, the object of knowledge is the processural dimensions of signification and experience. Second, there is a crisis of universalistic concepts like human nature, Englishness, and autonomous or transcendent aesthetic experience. Third, there is a crisis of authority regarding English and the humanities as sites claiming to disseminate civilizing, disinterested forms of knowledge. Finally, there is a crisis of valuation, the fact that cultural life is comprised of multiple, competing, and unequal sources of valuation made by differently situated social groups. There are therefore no longer consensually agreed-upon canonic texts—even Shakespeare is not immune in this regard. Nor is there an undisputed standard language or a "one-size-fits-all" curriculum, in spite of government attempts to secure such fictions.

All of these crises indelibly alter what counts as "doing English" for cultural studies, necessitating that English teachers engage in theory work. Of course, at one level, English teaching has always been about triangulating between curriculum guidelines, what's in the bookroom, what seems to "work" with a particular group of students, and one's own developing pedagogical-practical repertoire. But cultural studies asks that such links be made in more theoretically conscious and extensive ways: a fashioning of always contingent connections between a specific curricular project, one's values as a teacher, one's beliefs as a citizen, a group of texts to be explored, the theories that might inform them, one's perceptions of the desires and needs of students, pragmatic exercises intended to ground any enterprise at the classroom level, what working in this particular neighborhood involves, the demands of the wider social context and historical moment. This is asking a lot, I realize. But unless we consciously raise and debate these issues regularly not only with colleagues but with students, we are not engaging in cultural studies. As Kathleen McCormick (1992) states, "we are all always already theorists," since theory is inscribed in our habitual ways of asking questions, assumptions about what makes a worthwhile curriculum or a good answer. The only choice is "whether we and our students will be self-conscious . . . about the theories that guide our perceptions" or not (p. 114). Articles like Stuart Hall's (1992) "Cultural Studies and Its Theoretical Legacies" and John Storey's (1996) edited collection *What Is Cultural Studies?: A Reader* provide useful surveys of cultural studies theory in greater depth than I can here.

WHAT IS "CULTURE" IN CULTURAL STUDIES?

We use the word culture in two senses: to mean a whole way of life—the common meanings; [and also] to mean the arts and learning . . . . I insist on both, and on the significance of their conjunction. The questions I ask about our culture are questions about our general and common purposes, yet also questions about deep personal meanings. Culture is ordinary.
(Williams, 1989a, p. 4)

When we are at our most natural, our most everyday, we are also at our most cultural.
(Turner, 1992, p. 2)

The concept of culture in "cultural studies" does not simply designate what we traditionally associate with the school subject English; namely, literacy, the study of literature, competencies in written and verbal expression across a range of discourses and aesthetic experience. Nor is it separable from politics, economic factors, the traces of history, and mundane, everyday concerns. Indeed, the quotation by Turner above suggests cultural studies needs to pay attention to the everyday world and what is thought of as common sense since these are constituted and continuously reorganized by cultural processes like language and the media. The apparent naturalness of everyday life is therefore not left unproblematized by cultural studies. What appears self-evident, taken as obvious, can frequently be recovered as *myth* in Roland Barthes's sense of this term: ideologically invested signs masking the workings of power and history. In *Mythologies* (1973) and *The Eiffel Tower* (1979), Barthes proceeds to defamiliarize "what goes without saying," revealing for instance how tourist guides, wrestling matches, favorite meals, civic landmarks, examples in grammar textbooks, haircuts, and a variety of other seemingly innocent signs are caught up with the workings of power and social desire. I will return to *Mythologies* as a stimulus for practical work in the last section of this chapter. For now, I want to underline the value of Barthes's work in showing how subtle, materialized signifying processes are significant to the extent that they are crucial meaning-making practices in a society. Another way of putting this would be to say that Barthes explores the pedagogy of the everyday, showing how any attempt "to decipher the world's signs always means to struggle with a certain innocence" (1988, p. 158) if we are to disclose their "anonymous ideologies" (1973, p. 140).

Similarly, bell hooks (1997) has stated that "popular culture is where the pedagogy is." The curriculum of the English classroom must therefore be placed alongside the deluge of linguistic, iconic, and embodied signs in popular culture that now vie for students' attention. Both types of culture play a central role in how a society thinks about itself. A good reason for exploring cultural studies is the priority it accords to mundane semiotic processes as educative. All forms of culture are seen as "pedagogical" to the extent that they rewrite our sense of legitimate knowledge, subjectivity, and social relations (Giroux, 1992). Culture matters, suggests hooks, because it informs and shapes subjectivity and collectivity behind our backs and in dramatic ways. It is vital for English teachers to enter into a dialogue with prosaic everyday signs that are largely invisible and require a special effort to raise to critical visibility. Yet, since they are taken for granted—the water we now swim in—they inevitably provide the unstated contexts of the texts we teach: Shakespeare meets *The Simpsons;* today's news is always an intertext for classroom novels. However, criticism does not simply mean approaching everyday pedagogies as unredeemable, purely negative forces. Rather, it entails an open exploration of them as sites of social reproduction *and* experimentation, cultural expression *and* regulation, aesthetics *and* ideology, commerce *and* cultural performance. It thus requires forms of understanding and critique simultaneously.

The links between cultural studies and education go back a long way. In an address to teachers, Richard Hoggart (1989), one of the originators, noted that cultural studies has an "educational presence" in several ways (p. 11). First, as a recutting of educational space, it signaled discontent with traditional subject boundaries, providing a means of asking questions about culture that other disciplines frequently blocked. In this light, Nelson (1991) advises that cultural studies "is inescapably concerned with and critical of the politics of disciplinary knowledge" (p. 34). Indeed, taking up culture in all of its entangled messiness (e.g., events are turned into books that become movies that spawn a line of products and give rise to lived appropriations by groups who stage events, and so on) requires a dismantling of school "subjects" as we know them. Yet, even within English, cultural studies acts "as an irritant," taking on board literary concepts only to revise and put them to work in the service of a different agenda (Hall, 1990a, p. 18). Williams and Hoggart taught university extension courses to adults, reading and debating texts with students who insisted that learning speak to their own experiences, concerns, and everyday situations. Traditional subject boundaries were necessarily crossed in these encounters. Questions of pedagogy were thus central to the founding of cultural studies, forged in the context of postwar classrooms.

In contrast, the English classroom still tends to stage culture in polar terms. On the one hand, culture is a group of privileged texts (literature) or communicational processes—reading, writing, listening, speaking—without content; on the other hand, it is a species of infectious disease, exemplified by tabloids, prime-time television, or consumer culture. Familiarity with the first version of culture is believed to have emancipatory effects (e.g., literary insight, personal empowerment); exposure to the second leads variously to passivity, aggression, massification, and bad taste. The task of the English teacher in this context becomes that of inoculating students against the banal corruptions of everyday life. In contrast, cultural studies encourages educators to explore a wide range of cultural practices with their students in order to understand how they work; only then are they to be critiqued, remade, or revalued. The work that signs do subjectively and experientially is regarded as boundary-creating: "a conflictual set of practices of representation bound up with the processes of formation and re-formation of social groups" (Frow & Morris, 1996, p. 356).

In this sense, cultural studies is about what Homi Bhabha (1988) calls "the problem of the cultural" in its broadest sense (p. 19). This means analyzing how cultural practices "differentiate, discriminate, and authorize the production of fields of force, reference, applicability and capacity" (p. 18). Intimately caught up with identity at all levels, culture is explored as a dynamic play of signifying practices that creates versions of sameness and difference, both types of pleasure and forms of symbolic violence, and fosters someone's empowerment and someone else's exclusion—in one and the same act of representation. Cultural studies, then, as a way of engaging "the problem of the cultural," is about more than literary texts, language processes, or media education—though it is concerned with these things as well.

Additionally, culture is not just a good thing for cultural studies, but "must be seen as much for what it is not and for what it triumphs over . . . as for what it positively is" (Said, 1983, p. 11). An insistent theme of cultural studies, then, is that "culture" is comprised of a plurality of dividing practices whereby identities, events, and objects are constituted in relation to often unstated alterities and oppositions. Another way of putting this is to state that, at a primary level, this approach explores culture as the sphere of the inscription and enactment of social differences across a wide range of signifying processes. At another level, as Buck-Morss (1989) indicates, we will require a dialectical optic for reading culture, so that those who teach versions of "cultural heritage" via literature have to ask themselves not only about the positive features of literary traditions, but how can they become

> mindful of the violence in the wake of which these "treasures" have been gathered up and preserved, whereas others have disappeared, and countless others not even been created? . . . And more, can we view seriously, with reverence, the . . . material objects of mass culture as monuments of utopian hope of past [and present] generations, and to its betrayal? Who will teach these truths, and in what form will they be passed on to those who come after us? (p. 336)

The products of mass media and consumer culture must therefore be explored just as thoughtfully, positively, and critically as any Dickens novel. The latter, after all, were forms of popular culture in their day. Such reflections give rise to a necessary self-locating moment within cultural studies, about which I say more below. Here I want to stress that less authoritarian versions of teaching literary tradition or cultural heritage will need, paradoxically, to make clear their politics, that is, how their sense of the present is always a basic condition of a past text's legibility (p. 340).

As a way of pulling together a number of themes discussed so far, I end this section with a definition of cultural studies by its most articulate advocate, Stuart Hall. What his writing as a whole demonstrates is a critical approach to culture apprehended as an active, interlinked set of processes rather than static artifacts. Culture is more a verb than a noun for Hall, the meanings of any cultural form or practice requiring an understanding of its role within the network of social relations it is a part of. Or, as Grossberg, Nelson, and Treichler (1992) insist, "all forms of cultural production need to be studied in relation to other cultural practices and to social and historical structures" (p. 4). Here is Hall's (1996) definition:

> [*Cultural studies* is] concerned with the changing ways of life of societies and groups and the networks of meanings that individuals and groups use to make sense of and communicate with one another; what Raymond Williams once called whole ways of communicating, which are always whole ways of life; the dirty crossroads where popular culture intersects with the high arts; that place where power cuts across knowledge, or where cultural processes anticipate social change. . . . [It] reflects the rapidly shifting ground of thought knowledge, argument and debate about a society and about its own culture. . . . It represents something, indeed, of the weakening of the traditional boundaries among the disciplines and the growth of forms of interdisciplinary research that don't easily fit, or can't be contained within the confines of the existing divisions of knowledge. (pp. 336–337)

WHAT IS INVOLVED IN CULTURAL STUDIES ANALYSIS?

This description of the project of cultural studies indicates a politicization and a widening of the interpretive methods of English to include not only the dynamics of language but several interacting layers of meaning making. Fundamental to any cultural studies, Leitch (1992) argues, is a "protocol of entanglement," a way of conducting analysis in terms of linked temporal and spatial networks (p. 167). This requires drawing upon a diversity of methods: textual explication, institutional analysis, historical understanding, ethnographies of cultural use, and so forth. The cultural significance of any sign, object or practice can only be assessed therefore after an exploration of each of these dynamics as well as their mutual interaction. Meaning is constituted across a range of social relations; it is conjunctural.

For English teachers, this means texts need to be recovered as a moment

Figure 3.1. Three Circuits of Cultural Studies Concern

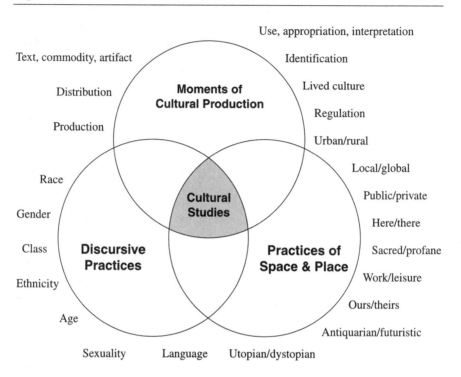

in a larger complex of social processes, many of which are inevitably institutional. The act of reinscribing cultural objects within the circuits that give them meaning does not, however, strip solitary artifacts of their active-reactive qualities. Texts, for example, are themselves acts that can make a difference in particular contexts, depending on how they in turn are performed or made to mean. Of course, methods of close textual reading already apprehend literature as the locus of active dynamics at work upon readers; conversely, reader-response models of English endow students with agency and creativity in their appropriation of texts. Yet the "larger complex of social processes" referred to above extends much wider than this for a cultural studies approach. One way that I have found useful of getting at this more extensive, relational model is to sketch three overlapping orbits of concern. (See Figure 3.1.)

According to Williams (1989b), the "central theoretical question in cultural analysis [is what are] the specific relationships through which works are made and move?" (p. 173). The point of analyzing culture in terms of the three circuits of concern outlined below is that they provide useful heuristic ways of thinking about culture in the conjunctural manner Williams recommends. The first circle, Moments of Cultural Production, asks how a specific text or artifact was initially produced and subsequently refunctioned (in which historical contexts? within what material constraints?). Next, it turns to questions regarding both the internal signifying dynamics of a text and the discourses it is installed within (as new cars are within advertising, social initiatives within policy documents, and school texts in curricular discourses). This also involves a calculation of the intertextual references and dialogues with other representations active at that same time. Additionally, questions are raised about how and by whom it was appropriated; to what uses was it put and to what ends; what types of identifications became invested in its use? Next, attention focuses on the role it may have played within a specific community, for example, in articulating its values, in shaping or redefining its active distinctions. And were such uses conscious, semiconscious, or largely unconscious? Of equal interest is whether this text was regulated (e.g., by law, commentary, implicit social norms), and whether the text itself became regulative (as policy documents or novels in school are—the latter becoming required, ritualized, examinary uses of language). In short, there is a rich set of questions to pursue within this circuit of concerns. For an in-depth example of this type of analysis, take a look at *Doing Cultural Studies: The Story of the Sony Walkman* (1997) by Du Gay, Hall, Janes, Mackay, and Negus.

My second orbit of concerns, Discursive Practices, overlaps with the first, but highlights the particular work of discourses, semiosis, and language as these processes create and enact versions of sameness and difference. For instance, how does a distinct use of language and imagery in a given popular film help to produce specific versions of what it means to be male or female, adolescent or elderly, Arab or Anglo-Saxon? This type of analysis assists us in a grounded awareness of what Hall (1996) means by claiming that culture is "the dirty crossroads . . . where power cuts across knowledge" (p. 336). One of the issues here is a practical understanding of how some discourses become dominant and others get subordinated, how they are reiterated and transformed in a culture and become implicated in people's lived experiences. The play of power, pleasure, and identity at the level of everyday signs is the central focus of this circuit of analysis.

Gramsci's statement that "history has deposited in each of us a set of traces but without an inventory" (quoted in Said, 1998) suggests another exciting but difficult set of tasks along this discursive axis of concern. What is involved, for example, in going beyond the surface of the personally meaningful and felt responses of students to an interesting text? It would seem to mean giving some thought to the systemic discourses that underpin their various interpretations. In this sense, cultural studies foregrounds the process of cultural interpretation itself, asking students and teachers to not only think about the circulation and use of texts, images, and commodities by others, but reflect on how our own social locations, perspectives, and interests affect our evaluations of cultural artifacts. Frow and Morris (1996) argue that "it is perhaps this self-situating and *limiting* moment of analysis that most clearly distinguishes work in cultural studies from other modes of analysis on which practitioners may draw" (p. 354). A self-reflexive stance is more than just an individual matter; it involves considering how our interpretations draw upon systemic discourses and social forms of understanding that are in turn nested within networks like those sketched in the diagram above. The point here is not simply to expose interpretations as "biased" or "distorted" because they are "influenced" by affective investments and systemic discourses. Rather, it is to illustrate how the latter make understanding possible in the first place, how they constitute its very ground. This view holds that interpretation is always a transformation of one language by another. Students can only grasp how this process works if you explore both sides of its dynamics with them. These arguments point to another reason why full analytical closure is impossible in cultural studies, although specific interpretations may give rise to ethical actions—as they should if we are to make a difference in the world. The range of issues here is extensive. McCormick's *The Culture of Reading and the Teaching of English* (1994), Hall and Du Gay's *Questions of Cultural Identity* (1996), and Canaan and Epstein's *A Question of Discipline: Teaching Cultural Studies* (1997) explore in greater depth the complex pedagogical and discursive themes gestured by this circuit of concerns.

Finally, and most frequently neglected in cultural analysis, there is the spatial matrix within which cultural and discursive processes occur. As Hall (1990b) eloquently states, "discourse and culture is placed" (p. 223). In Grossberg's (1993) terms, we need to explore how signifying practices help to establish "geographies of becoming" (p. 9). My third circuit of concerns, Spatial Practices, therefore raises questions about the ways in which culture, in its differentiating movement, creates versions of here and away, public and private space, proper and illicit zones, sacred and profane places, urban and rural landscapes, work and leisure spaces, center and periphery, the local and the global, antiquated and utopian spaces—to name just a few of the types of sites any culture enacts. This third circle asks us to (literally) ground culture, investigating it as a repertoire of place-making activities (Dear, 1997). A key principle here is that space is more than just a passive container of people, things, and discourses. It is both a social product and itself a distinct means of producing the social. Indeed, to a great extent power can be understood as the ability to turn space into place (Berland, 1997, p. 79), that is, to constrain the spatial dimensions of becoming, to initiate versions of social order, and to shape the ground on which social possibilities and meanings emerge. In this light, school buildings can be thought of as "material classifying devices" (Markus, 1993, p. 19), organizing categories of knowledge, learners by age and ability, and the types of interaction possible within them.

Relevant therefore are a whole range of questions about the links between space, signs, and power: for example, regarding representations of space, spatial practices, histories of a specific place, and the "mattering maps" people navigate by or use to bond to particular locations so that they become "places of belonging" (Grossberg, 1991, p. 25). "Topography" literally means to write a place. Novels and poems are well known for writing space, that is, creating unique senses of place: Dickens's London, Hardy's Wessex, or, in a Canadian context, Laurence's Manawaka, Mitchell's prairie towns, and Montgomery's P.E.I. come to mind. English teachers are already familiar with literature's extensive use of geographical metaphors as a way of raising and linking social, ethical, and political questions. However, reading texts through a neighborhood lens, as Moshenberg (1996) suggests, means "tak[ing] our geographies seriously . . . a matter of where we stand and how we . . . articulate the sites of our standings" in terms of our own locations as well as the neighborhoods students live within and against which texts are inevitably deciphered (p. 89). Similarly, media educators often stress the importance of electronic media in shaping an awareness of "us" versus "them," the neighborhood and the nation, the local and the global. In the same vein, advertisements, television newscasts, soap operas, films, and so forth can all be seen as mapping fantasies. Taken as a whole, electronic media are radically new social environments and powers over space. The task for teachers and students who explore this third circuit of concerns is therefore that of figuring out the "deeper systems of space that are at work in any text" (Jameson, 1994, p. 50), and the space-binding, space-fragmenting qualities of different media practices (Innis, 1986). Once again, the issues here are extensive, and texts like J. H. Miller's *Topographies* (1995), J. Donald's "This, Here, Now: Imagining the Modern City" (1997), G. Benko and U. Strohmayer's *Space and Social Theory* (1997), and K. Hetherington's *The Badlands of Modernity* (1997) do them more justice than I can here.

CULTURAL STUDIES IN THE ENGLISH CLASSROOM: GENERAL CONSIDERATIONS

What I have tried to sketch in the previous section is something of the synthesizing impulse of cultural studies, its manner of conceiving of cultural events, objects, and practices in terms of the "constituting and dissolving relations" that give them meaning (Nelson, 1991, p. 32). This approach is not so much a rejection of the concerns of English teaching as it is their displacement and modification by a more politicized framework interested in exploring all forms of cultural production. Since the relations that need to be considered have multiplied for this model, it seems that English teachers must now become part historian, part sociologist, part philosopher, part political theorist, and so forth, in addition to their usual areas of expertise, language and literature. This is true to the extent that cultural studies is a theory of contexts; that is, it asks what counts as context in particular situations: the specific relations that make a delimited cultural practice meaningful for the various communities that produce, participate in, or are affected by it. Yet this crisis of more (more contexts, more theory, more self-reflective interpretation) is part of the price cultural studies educators have to pay in order to reconnect culture to the public sphere and to break out of the confining, fragmented approaches of most school subjects.

Another answer is that the whole pill doesn't have to be swallowed all at once. For any concrete analysis, some moments, questions, and connections are inevitably more relevant than others. In a specific case study of a cultural process, the needs and interests of students also determine which relations are pertinent and which, for the present, become peripheral. Another factor at work here, as McRobbie (1984) states, is the fact that cultural studies is not so much about establishing rigorous "causal links" between moments in the circuits I have described. Instead, she insists,

> the emphasis is placed on establishing loose sets of relations, capillary actions and movements, a spilling out among and between different fields: work and leisure, fact and fiction, and fantasy and reality, individual and social experience. (p. 142)

Finally, there is the small matter of what can actually be done in the particular English department, local community, or classroom where English teachers find themselves. Ministry policies, curriculum guidelines, and textbooks may establish the broad framework of "doing English," but local administrators, other English teachers, students, and parents determine how restrictively or creatively these boundaries are interpreted. Also, teachers should not underestimate the extent to which they may encounter resistance to the new theoretical languages, social grammars, and cross-disciplinary questions that their approaches will involve. Experiments with cultural studies almost always experience some version of these constraints. In this light, a colleague once remarked that "cultural studies is anything you can get away with" given claustrophobic disciplinary structures and the pressures of particular work environments (Fortier, 1992, p. 312). This is not a matter of disguising what one intends to do so much as finding opportunities to use existing curricula for this wider analysis. It means taking seriously official rhetoric about interdisciplinarity, "integrated learning," or "holistic education" so that the project of cultural studies might emerge: to get students to see the world around them as a social construction, one that is changeable and open to their meanings.

Given these Polonius-like caveats, some of the most interesting work students produce (I also teach media and English courses) comes out of cultural studies projects like those described below. Returning to the earlier discussion of Barthes's *Mythologies*, for example, I use this text as a jumping off point for cultural studies work in a couple of ways. After an initial discussion of the text as a whole, we analyze and collectively rewrite a specific Barthian myth. Those on wrestling, the Blue Guide, or Dominici are useful because they invite immediate comparisons, respectively, to contemporary television wrestling, current forms of tourism, and the most recent media hero or scapegoat. Next, I assign students the task of individually decoding and producing a modern "myth" of their own choosing. A recent sample of these included items on bottled water, four-wheel all-terrain vehicles, air miles cards, *Wired* magazine, Roots clothing, Canadian weather forecasts, and a popular film. As an initial cultural studies assignment, it also has the advantage of marrying the theoretical to the concrete since Barthes's text itself moves between these poles.

But there is another way to begin. As Frow and Morris (1996) suggest, rather than starting from a specific book, cultural studies can just as easily start from

> the particular, the detail, the scrap of ordinary or banal existence, and then work[s] to unpack the density of relations and of intersecting social domains that inform it. Rather than being interested in television or architecture or pinball machines in themselves . . . it tends to be interested in the way such apparatuses work as points of concentration of social meaning, as "media" literally, the carriers of all the complex and conflictual practices of sociality. (p. 354)

FILE OF CULTURAL (UN)CERTAINTIES

An assignment that I use in my graduate cultural studies course might help to make this approach clearer. Early in the class, I inform students that doing cultural studies involves a critical respeaking of theory, making it one's own by applying it to local contexts and felt problems. They are therefore asked to assemble a "file of cultural (un)certainties" during the term on some specific practice, problem, question, or dilemma that intrigues them within contemporary culture. The idea is to set up a dialogue between the theory they read during the course and a specific set of objects or cultural phenomenon of their choice. They are to use the file as a way of interrogating the theory, and to employ the theory as a toolkit playing across the file to see what it reveals of the dynamics at work there. I encourage them to undertake this assignment in groups, though picking something of personal interest also means some students will inevitably work individually. Collaborative group work of this kind, involving moving back and forth between course readings, small-group discussions, and research and reading agendas customized to serve a specific project on a cultural text or practice, is a long-standing tradition in cultural studies (cf. Johnson, 1997, pp. 454–455).

I also explain that the term *(un)certainties* is meant to signal that what they explore should be ambiguous, contradictory, and complex enough so that lines of inquiry remain relatively open, even though they may already have some clear ("certain") insights on it. Besides found artifacts illustrating different aspects of their chosen phenomenon, the file must include some of their own writing to indicate the overall project, their analysis of specific items collected, and how they might be interrelated. Near the end of term each group presents their file, outlining the project, discussing artifacts, and providing their overall analysis. They end by posing their ongoing questions for further research in this area. They are also invited to reflect on differences in interpretation within the group, and between the group and other (e.g., primary) users of these texts and artifacts. This last task helps to ground the earlier claim that cultural studies work should include a self-situating moment since it is here that they make clear that neither their choice of what to study nor their interpretations of it are innocent. As Walkerdine (1990) demonstrates in an important cultural studies article, people always bring to their inquiries and interpretations layers of discursive inculturation, social histories, and personal desires.

Finally, the rest of the class enters the discussion of the file and the issues it generates. What I look for in presentations is the extent to which groups make visible the conjunctures and historical relations at work in the cultural practices they investigate. By the end of each session, I want the class to have a fuller sense of how this practice or text functions as "a multiple and mobile field of force relations," in Foucault's sense (1979, p. 102), or, drawing on terms used earlier, how it is an intersection of signifying practices, forms of subjectivity, institutional structures, and networks of power. A tall order! Yet, over the past year, many projects stand out as exemplary: on the Body Shop, designer clothing, Caribbean tourism, café culture in Toronto, Asian Dub music, the boom in backyard gardening, the novels of Toni Morrison, computer ads on television, toys children bring to school, the Oprah Winfrey show, social work textbooks, shock-talk radio shows, the Spice Girls, romance novels, lesbian and gay urban spaces, Maple Leaf Gardens, and representations of fear, panic, and anxiety in mainstream media. Taken together, such projects demonstrate that the real object of cultural studies is "itself a kind of . . . web with all kinds of unexpected linkages, vicinities, identities, though with differences and hidden elements too" (Johnson, 1997, p. 469).

"I HAVE COME TO TAKE MY PLACE . . ."

Adapting the previous exercise for high school use, I would meet groups more frequently than with graduate students, help them clarify their focus, build a relevant vocabulary for a specific analysis, establish a research and reading agenda with some accessible theoretical articles if available, and generally push them to account for all relevant aspects of the phenomenon they are investigating. But there is much more at stake in the "unexpected linkages, vicinities, identities . . . and hidden elements" students may want to explore and in the discoveries they are likely to make in this process. While writing this chapter, news of the carnage at Columbine High stuns me when I turn on the radio. An article in this morning's newspaper states one of the killers, Dylan Klebold, "read a lyrical essay he had written on a gun fair out loud in English class" the week before the massacre and "got a good mark for it, but no one saw what was underneath" (Mitchell, 1999, p. A16). His partner, Eric Harris, maintained a Web site containing apocalyptic, hate-saturated verse, which included the lines, "I have come to take my place . . . I am your unexpectedness" (p. A16). Another story speculates that Hollywood movies like *Heathers, Natural Born Killers,* or *The Basketball Diaries* may have supplied the "media models" for the killers' actions (Houpt, 1999, p. A16), while a third speaks in medical and psychological terms of counseling for violent or alienated youth (Barber, 1999, p. A19).

What, if anything, can cultural studies possibly have to say about such life and death matters? In offering students a chance to explore the social, ethical, and political implications of cultural practices important to them or evident in their communities, it inevitably provides opportunities for the "unleashing of unpopular things" like racism, chauvinism, and other raw tensions (Britzman, 1991). Yet, surely it is better to address such issues directly than, as with Klebold's English essay, to ignore the symbolic, discursive, even "lyrical" performances of anger, mark them for form alone, and let them fester until they explode. What cultural studies pedagogy makes possible is a chance to explore with students the network of signifying practices that inform their identities-under-construction.

In school subcultures like "the black trenchcoat mafia," for example, there were complex articulations at work: black boots, clothing, and makeup; neo-Nazi insignia; Goth rock music; video war games; right-wing and fascist Internet sites; gun culture; popular racist discourses; forms of aggressive masculinity; middle-class family and neighborhood structures in suburban America; patterns of difference operating in this particular school (e.g., "jocks" versus "Goths")—and so on. The meanings of such clusters are not given in advance, nor do individual items within them always bear their significance ready and waiting to be read on the surface. The film *Heathers,* for example, can just as easily be interpreted as an ironic indictment of violence. Nor can clusters be understood without examining the signs, practices, and values they were in conflict with, that "they were just so different" from (Mitchell, 1999, p. A16)—the problematic mainstream culture within this school. What is required, then, is an interpretation of how cultural elements get used and renegotiated, how they are articulated and then coalesce at specific sites to forge versions of social difference—in the case of Columbine High, versions that could kill, the paradox that "taking one's place" meant attempting to annihilate a place altogether. Overall, cultural studies shifts the emphasis away from isolated representations and practices per se and toward the network of relationships that make something meaningful in a given context. It would also have problems with behavioristic models of automatic media effects, or the stigmatization of "alienated youth" in isolation from the community norms they transgress. Cultural studies thus means teachers and students working collaboratively to understand the continuous cultural "production of relations . . . never guaranteed in advance" (Grossberg, 1993) that, taken together, comprise a community. All of this, of course, won't by itself stop the tragedy of a Columbine High. It will, however, make it harder to claim "no one saw" or contemplated what was at stake in the differences on display there.

There are many other kinds of projects that open up a space for cultural studies within English. I would include here moves toward contrapuntal reading (e.g., Conrad's *Heart of Darkness* placed beside Achebe's *Things Fall Apart*) and radial reading (setting historical, theoretical, political, popular, or other kinds of texts alongside literary ones). Both of these approaches promote cross-disciplinary dialogue and intercultural exchange. Verdecchia's play, *Fronteras Americanas* (1993), explicitly juxtaposes popular media stereotypes and lived experience within a Canadian context—an example of contrapuntal dynamics within a single text. Especially relevant, as the files students selected indicate, are efforts to explore communicational practices English traditionally marginalizes: popular and media representations; new and old technologies such as video games, tabloids, magazines, telephones, the Internet; and mundane community, policy, or educational texts. For example, old textbooks gathering dust in school bookrooms or outdated ministry guidelines can be examined for what they reveal about doing English in the past. Taken on as a group project, students can get a glimpse of the shifting values in English and thus an opportunity to see it as a social construction. Small-scale group research, like interviewing a sample of tabloid users to discover their reading practices, can rebound in turn on classroom awareness, sensitizing students to their own modes of appropriation, reading, and interpretation.

Practices that move between theory and collaborative cultural remaking are especially important. As Medway (1996) argues, the act of making or refashioning material signs in whatever form—texts, images, clothing, the built environment, and so forth—is a way of participating in "the public space of appearance" and thus of potentially making a difference to one's local community since one is dealing in the "currency" of public culture. Such exercises can function as a powerful means of students knowing themselves concretely and socially. Teachers, however, may have to provide the moments of theoretical provocation in this process, insisting on a constant oscillation between theory and practice, critique and making. Both Buckingham (1994) and Cohen (1998) demonstrate the need for this kind of continuous dialogue and conceptual development if a project is to call itself cultural studies. There are even ways of returning to the canon but with a cultural studies' difference, evident, for example, in Fortier's (1992) work on Shakespeare, Tompkins' (1994) study of Hawthorne, McCarthy et al.'s (1995) consideration of Morrison's novels, or Nelson's (1994a; 1994b) theoretically charged, contrapuntal use of poetry.

What makes any of these exercises cultural studies and not something else is their refusal of formalist, instrumental models of studying language or culture in favor of accounts that stress the politics of the sign and a consideration of how signifying processes produce our ways of knowing and living. While this conception of culture can frequently be justly criticized for its imprecision and ambitious reach, it also represents the need to make questions about signification more relevant to people's lives and learning. On an experiential level, English teaching can demand one's identity, a constant immersion in language work, texts, and student responses to them. This intense context, as rewarding as it is, doesn't automatically make for a historical or theoretical critique of the constraining categories of knowledge or dominant teaching paradigms in our subject, nor of the severe limits of attending to language and print in isolation from the other cultural processes they are now caught up by. Some of these ways of framing our work were built into the subject from its birth. Marked, for example, by homogeneity in its very name and arising within imperialist logics, English is still largely based on notions of national, individualistic, ethnic, and racial versions of identity (Morgan, 1997; Morrison, 1992).

To end where I began, then, with Williams: sometimes "the most basic concepts . . . from which we begin, are seen to be not concepts but problems, not analytic problems either, but historical movements that are still unresolved" (quoted in Green, 1982, pp. 77–78). In effect, Williams invites us to make English historically peculiar, to recognize that our subject is often characterized by a set of naturalized categories (literature), taken-for-granted routines (character sketches), reified concepts (theme), and overly precise genres (the essay). Although these conceptual resources and ways of framing knowledge were originally responsive to the historical conditions they emerged within, many have now become problematic. The diagram I sketched earlier, therefore, can also be applied to the subject of English as a moment of cultural production in its own right, a way of privileging of some discourses on culture over others, and a spatially segregated "domain" of knowledge with its own "department." In the end, what cultural studies has to offer English teaching are some urgent postdisciplinary questions about the connections between signifying practices, communities, and power. Making English's boundaries permeable in this fashion represents nothing less than a historically pertinent and creative rethinking of our subject so that it can address the ethical, political, and pedagogical dimensions of contemporary cultural practices.

REFERENCES

Barber, J. (1999, April 22). MDs surprised more outbreaks do not erupt. *The Globe and Mail*, p. A19.

Barthes, R. (1973). *Mythologies*. London: Paladin.

Barthes, R. (1979). *The Eiffel Tower and other mythologies* (R. Howard, Trans.). New York: Hill & Wang.

Barthes, R. (1988). *The semiotic challenge* (R. Howard, Trans.). New York: Hill & Wang.

Bell, A. M. (1879). *On teaching reading in public schools*. Brantford, ON: Thomas Henderson.

Bell, D. C., & Bell, A. M. (1882). *Bell's standard elocutionist*. London: Hodder & Stoughton.

Benko, G., & Strohmayer, U. (Eds.). (1997). *Space and social theory*. Oxford: Blackwell.

Bennett, T. (1991). Coming out of English: A Policy calculus for cultural studies. In K. Ruthven (Ed.), *Beyond the disciplines: The new humanities*. Canberra, Australia: Highland Press.

Berland, J. (1997, Spring). Space at the margins. *Topia*, *1*, 55–82.

Bhabha, H. (1988, Summer). The commitment to theory. *New Formations*, *5*, 5–23.

Britzman, D. (1991). Decentering discourses in teacher education: Or, the unleashing of unpopular things. *Journal of Education*, *173*(3), 60–80.

Buck-Morss, S. (1989). *The dialectics of seeing*. Cambridge, MA: MIT Press.

Buckingham, D. (1994). Solving the theoretical problem? Positive images and practical work. In D. Buckingham (Ed.), *Cultural studies goes to school* (pp. 184–210). London: Taylor & Francis.

Canaan, J., & Epstein, D. (Eds.). (1997). *A question of discipline: Teaching cultural studies*. Boulder, CO: Westview Press.

Cohen, P. (1998). Tricks of the trade: On teaching arts and "race" in the classroom. In D. Buckingham (Ed.), *Teaching popular culture: Beyond radical pedagogy* (pp. 153–176). Bristol, U.K.: UCL Press.

Dear, M. (1997). Postmodern bloodlines. In G. Benko & U. Strohmayer (Eds.), *Space and social theory* (pp. 49–71). Oxford: Blackwell.

Donald, J. (1997). This, here, now: Imagining the modern city. In S. Westwood & J. Williams (Eds.), *Imagining cities, scripts, signs, memory* (pp. 181–201). London: Routledge.

Du Gay, P., Hall, S., Janes, L., Mackay, H., & Negus, K. (1997). *Doing cultural studies: The story of the Sony Walkman*. London: Sage.

Eagleton, T. (1991). The enemy within. *English in Education*, *25*(3), 3–9.

Fortier, M. (1992). Reteaching Shakespeare. In J. Berlin & M. Vivion (Eds.), *Cultural studies in the English classroom* (pp. 312–322). Portsmouth, NH: Boynton/Cook.

Foucault, M. (1979). *The history of sexuality* (Vol. 1). London: Penguin.

Frow, J. (1992). Beyond the disciplines: Cultural studies. In K. Ruthven (Ed.), *Beyond the disciplines: The new humanities*. Canberra, Australia: Highland Press.

Frow, J., & Morris, M. (1996). Australian cultural studies. In J. Storey (Ed.), *What is cultural studies?: A reader* (pp. 344–367). New York: St. Martin's Press.

Giroux, H. (1992). Series forward: Education, pedagogy and the politics of cultural work. In D. Trend (Ed.), *Cultural pedagogy*. New York: Bergin & Garvey.

Green, M. (1982). The centre for contemporary cultural studies. In P. Widdowson (Ed.), *Rereading English* (pp. 77–90). London: Methuen.

Grossberg, L. (1991). From media to popular culture. *Metro, 86,* 20–26.

Grossberg, L. (1993). Cultural studies and in new worlds. *Critical studies in mass communications, 10*(1), 1–22.

Grossberg, L. (1996). The circulation of cultural studies. In J. Storey (Ed.), *What is cultural studies?: A reader* (pp. 178–186). New York: St. Martin's Press.

Grossberg, L., Nelson, C., & Treichler, P. (Eds.). (1992). *Cultural studies.* New York: Routledge.

Hall, S. (1990a, Summer). The emergence of cultural studies and the crisis of the humanities. *October, 53,* 11–23.

Hall, S. (1990b). Cultural identity and diaspora. In J. Rutherford (Ed.), *Identity, community, culture, difference* (pp. 222–237). London: Lawrence & Wishart.

Hall, S. (1992). Cultural studies and its theoretical legacies. In L. Grossberg, C. Nelson, & P. Treichler (Eds.), *Cultural studies* (pp. 277–294). New York: Routledge.

Hall, S. (1996). Race, culture and communications: Looking backwards and forward at cultural studies. In J. Storey (Ed.), *What is cultural studies?: A reader* (pp. 336–343). New York: St. Martin's Press.

Hall, S., & Du Gay, P. (1996). *Questions of cultural identity.* London: Sage.

Hetherington, K. (1997). *The badlands of modernity.* London: Routledge.

Hoggart, R. (1989, Summer). Cultural studies in a strong state. *The English Magazine, 22,* 10–14.

hooks, b. (1997). *Cultural criticism and transformation* [Video]. Toronto: Kinetic Video.

Houpt, S. (1999, April 22). Some see eerie links with Hollywood's *Heather's. The Globe and Mail,* pp. A1, A16.

Innis, H. (1986). *Empire and communications.* Victoria, BC: Press Porcépic.

Jameson, F. (1994). Spatial systems in *North by Northwest.* In S. Zizek (Ed.), *Everything you always wanted to know about Lacan . . . but were afraid to ask Hitchcock* (pp. 47–72). London: Verso.

Johnson, R. (1997). Reinventing cultural studies: Remembering the best version. In J. Canaan & D. Epstein (Eds.), *A question of discipline: Teaching cultural studies* (pp. 452–488). Boulder, CO: Westview Press.

Kennedy, A. (1992). Committing the curriculum and other misdemeanors. In J. Berlin & M. Vivion (Eds.), *Cultural studies in the English classroom* (pp. 24–46). Portsmouth, NH: Boynton/Cook.

Kress, G. (1995). *Writing the future: English and the making of a culture of innovation.* London: National Association of Teachers of English.

Leitch, V. (1992). *Cultural criticism, literary theory and poststructuralism.* New York: Columbia University Press.

Markus, T. (1993). *Buildings and power.* London: Routledge.

McCarthy, C., David, S., Supriya, K., Wilson-Brown, C., Rodriquez, A., & Godina, H. (1995). The hypocrisy of incompleteness: Toni Morrison and the conception of the other. *Cultural Studies, 9*(2), 247–255.

McCormick, K. (1992). Always already theorists: Literary theory and theorizing in the undergraduate curriculum. In M. Kecht (Ed.), *Pedagogy is politics* (pp. 111–131). Urbana: University of Illinois Press.

McCormick, K. (1994). *The culture of reading and the teaching of English*. Manchester, UK: Manchester University Press.

McRobbie, A. (1984). Dance and social fantasy. In A. McRobbie & M. Nava (Eds.), *Gender and generation* (pp. 130–161). Houndsmills, Hampshire, England: Macmillan.

Medway, P. (1996). Representation and making: Student production in English. *Changing English*, *3*(2), 131–146.

Miller, J. H. (1995). *Topographies*. Stanford, CA: Stanford University Press.

Mitchell, A. (1999, April 22). Creepy duo favoured swastikas and lipstick. *The Globe and Mail*, pp. A1, A16.

Morgan, R. (1997). Messing with Mr. In-between: Multiculturalism and hybridization. *English Quarterly*, *28*(4)/*29*(1), 66–75.

Morrison, T. (1992). *Playing in the dark: Whiteness and the literary imagination*. Cambridge, MA: Harvard University Press.

Moshenberg, D. (1996). Standing in this neighborhood: Of English studies. In J. Slevin & A. Young (Eds.), *Critical theory and the teaching of literature* (pp. 75–92). Urbana, IL: National Council of Teachers of English.

Nelson, C. (1991). Always already cultural studies: Two conferences and a manifesto. *Journal of the Midwest (Modern Language Association)*, *24*(1), 24–38.

Nelson, C. (1994a). The cultural work of teaching noncanonical poetry. In D. Downing (Ed.), *Changing classroom practices* (pp. 53–72). Urbana, IL: National Council of Teachers of English.

Nelson, C. (1994b). A theorized poetry class. In D. Sadoff & W. Cain (Eds.), *Teaching contemporary theory to undergraduates* (pp. 179–191). New York: Modern Language Association.

Said, E. (1983). *The world, the text, the critic*. Cambridge, MA: Harvard University Press.

Said, E. (1998). *Edward Said on Orientalism* [Video]. Northampton, MA: Media Education Foundation.

Story, J. (Ed.). (1996). *What is cultural studies?: A reader*. New York: St. Martin's Press.

Tompkins, J. (1994). Masterpiece theatre: The politics of Hawthorne's literary reputation. In D. Richter (Ed.), *Falling into theory* (pp. 119–128). Boston: Bedford Books.

Turner, G. (1992). *British cultural studies: An introduction*. New York: Routledge.

Walkerdine, V. (1990). Video replay. In M. Alvarado & J. Thompson (Eds.), *The media reader* (pp. 339–357). London: British Film Institute.

Williams, R. (1975). *The long revolution*. Westport, CT: Greenwood Press.

Williams, R. (1989a). Culture is ordinary. In R. Williams (Ed.), *Resources of hope*. London: Verso. (Original work published 1958)

Williams, R. (1989b). The uses of cultural theory. In R. Williams (Ed.), *The politics of modernism* (pp. 163–176). London: Verso.

CHAPTER 4

Passionate Contracts: Discursive Contradiction and Struggle in Secondary English Teacher Education Programs

Ursula A. Kelly
Memorial University of Newfoundland

It is oftentimes enticing to see change simplistically, as the result of innovations in curriculum and pedagogy brought about by efforts to match better educational practice with societal changes and student needs. However, what is less often acknowledged is how efforts to effect change are never neutral or natural; change, like the world its effects reshape, is political. This chapter focuses on the contentious and deeply sedimented relationships of power, knowledge, desire, and identity, as they are constituted within beginning teachers themselves, as a means to examine how—and in what ways—change might be possible. In so doing, I argue that such constituted relationships are not sidebars in the work of teacher education, but are, instead, at its very heart, shaping how teachers work and how the work of teaching is envisioned, struggled over, and realized.

INTRODUCTION

Beginning teaching, or what is more commonly referred to as student teaching or practice teaching, is an especially provocative time when those who have chosen teaching as a contingent lifework face a multiplicity of struggles central to defining themselves in relation to the professional work of teaching. In this sense, it might be said that beginning teaching—that time in a teacher education program where students are introduced to and begin the practice of classroom teaching—is a central and galvanizing moment in the negotiation of teacher identity. For this reason, it is an experience to which those involved in teacher education should pay particular attention, for what is negotiated within beginning teaching is central to how previous beliefs about and future initiatives in teaching might be understood, provoked, and redefined.

In this chapter my purpose article is to focus explicitly on beginning teachers of secondary English and our work together to analyze the negotiation of teacher identity within a specific curriculum subject, English, and the troubling brought to bear on being a "club member," an English teacher. My focus is the delineation of a process through which to examine the "Englishes" over which these beginning teachers struggle, the nature of these struggles, and the implications of these struggles for how English studies courses are structured and taught within secondary teacher education programs. My concern is not with presenting ethnographic data of student voices but rather with theorizing ways and means by which voices may be accentuated, challenged, and politically analyzed. In short, I aim to suggest a process by which beginning teachers of secondary English might come to understand and to question the dynamics of knowledge, power, desire, and identity as *embodied relations*, as much about who these teachers are and where they have been as about what it is they wish to become. In so doing, I also suggest how analysis of such issues might urge a reconceptualization of teacher education generally.

A teacher education course in secondary English studies, wedged as it is between expectations of government departments of education as defined through curriculum guidelines and teacher certification requirements and the definitional, normative character of English as it is usually taught in public schools, can be a contradictory educational site. If the goals of a secondary English studies course are to provide both advances in and critiques of educational practices as they relate to the curriculum subject English, then such goals can conflict with the goals of the curriculum and those of many professional English teachers: The former mandates a curricular vision; the latter negotiates a set of preferred practices for the daily realities of schools from within (or aside from) that vision.

In such a scenario, a beginning teacher is positioned within a complex, contradictory, and conflicted trajectory. Pulled in various directions, such a teacher must begin to negotiate and reconcile the expectations of the curriculum, the profession, the teacher education program, and any personal hopes and dreams of what English teaching is, could, or should be. Within teacher education, there are two common approaches to this situation, each of which involves a form of denial or refusal of the difficult issues at hand. The first approach defines the purpose of a secondary English studies course in line with the expectations of provincial curricula. In this approach, a secondary English studies course has a technicist base and is developed to provide beginning teachers an array of "methods" by which to implement the current curriculum. The second approach ignores the existence of curricular direction and professional practices, proceeding with advances in English education as if the status quo did not exist. Each of these approaches has it own myopia; each ignores the need for the beginning teacher to maneuver competing expectations, as each also, and simultaneously, refuses the opportunity for positive change in which teacher education can participate.

Rather than ignore these conflicted expectations, it would be more educationally sound—and more helpful to beginning teachers—to approach such conflicts and contradictions as productive tensions through which beginning teachers might learn to become better teachers or from which they might gain a greater opportunity to envision the kind of teacher they might want to become. Such a focus requires not only the examination but also the heightening of these conflicts and contradictions. Such a focus also requires locating the choice of English "method" within a political vision, that is, seeing method as both suggesting and supporting a cultural politics.

ENGLISH ROMANTICIZED

For most beginning teachers of secondary English, the decision to teach is about many things, among them the desires to work with young people, to effect change in schools, to contribute to a community life, and to participate in a meaningful profession. Yet, in a profound and often unnamed way, the choice to teach is also, perhaps even more so, about an intimate, often passionate, relationship with English, that subject within which they desire to teach. Elsewhere (Kelly 1993b), I have written of the "missionary zeal" which can sometimes characterize expressions of this relationship to English. Here, I want to attend to the relationship of beginning teachers to their subject, or to a particular version of their subject, as a powerful dynamic in their evolving vision of teaching, both in terms of what is envisioned as possible to achieve within English and what (or who) it is possible to be(come) within English teaching.

At a fundamental level, what is captured in a relationship to a subject is a relationship to knowledge, what one perceives it to be, how one perceives it is generated and how one perceives its personal and social value. If, among other things, pedagogy is about knowledge, power, and audience, then a long-term relationship to a subject carries with it already formulated pedagogical assumptions about what counts as knowledge, for whom it is intended, and how it might be shared. Beginning teachers of English do carry with them such assumptions based on years of experience in, and often devotion to, a subject throughout their own elementary, secondary, and tertiary schooling. Given its intimate place in their own biographies, then, this relationship to English (and its implicit pedagogical assumptions) is less a self-attachment, a part, and more a self-embodiment, an intricate, integrative, and intimate part of who they are, how they see themselves and others, and what they hope and dream. In a manner, then, these are bodies onto which English has already scripted. Such embodiment shows itself in already established gestures toward texts and fashions of reading, in a penchant for criticism and a particular taste for culture, and in how an eye discerns and an ear hears: an overall cultural style, as it were. This style constitutes the starting point of a pedagogy about to go public and professional. This style is about a relationship to (English) knowledge that is about desire and identity: past traces, present longings, future urges.

The crucial point here is not so much how such apparent abstractions as knowledge, power, and pedagogy are, after all, fundamentally personal (and political), but rather how such personalized narratives—stories of embodied formations—may be rendered social, and disrupted and interrogated in the process. On the strength of their idealism alone, many of these stories convey a romanticized notion of the teaching of English. For those within teacher education, it is important to ask how such romanticized notions or "impossible dreams" of English might become "dreams of the possible" within English. How might the energy of investments in such romanticized notions be rechannelled as expressions of transformative human agency, expressions in which passion is well, not ill, placed?

Such questioning, which entails a wrestling with and a rethinking of our relationships to knowledge, is necessarily disruptive and discomfiting. It is also, arguably, what critical education is—or should be—about. Deborah Britzman (1998) clarifies what is at issue:

> Because learning is fundamentally about one's attachment to and disillusionment in knowledge, the force of learning is analogous to the force of affect and therefore charged with libidinal energy. We are as susceptible to knowledge as we are to the demands of others. We fall in and out of love with knowledge. Knowledge has the capacity to tear us apart, attempt repair, and become sublime to our thoughts. Like matters of love, learning interferes with the subject; or, put differently, when one learns, one is interfering with the self and her relations and positions in the social. (p. 53)

This manner in which knowledge poses a threat to identity is writ large as students engage discursive struggles in English. As teacher educators, such struggles are also implicated in our own histories with subject English. I have written previously (Kelly 1993a, 1997) about the terms and terrain—the modes of intervention—which map the shifts within my own relationship to English and its teaching. My own marks on the sad continuum of idealism and despair trace a personal and pedagogical struggle that is ongoing—and is reinvested with each new class of secondary English studies. Such reinvestments are also part of what transpires in the complex dynamic that constitutes a secondary English studies class.

A GEOGRAPHY OF ENGLISH?

Wendy Morgan (1997) writes of developing "a geography of English" (p. 1), an account of the subject that demonstrates "viewpoints from various topographical sites" (p. 1) as opposed to (but without dismissing) other metaphors (such as "historical overview"). While its preoccupation with topography is limiting, this geography metaphor is useful because it provides a sense in which position—where one stands and where one chooses to stand—shapes perspective, namely what one is able to see, to acknowledge, and to envision. Such an emphasis on the interrelationship of position and perspective also underscores how teaching is an ethical, political practice. Herein, I am also interested in how particular positions and perspectives are constituted (as desirable or not), how one comes to envision English in particular ways, and how a revisioning of English might be realized. Framed in this way, what I am attempting is a cartography of educational investment, a partial mapping of the strange and contradictory geography of internal landscapes (the *sub*ography) and educational expeditions as they relate to felt convictions and envisioned practices within the teaching of English.

Several such maps or schema like that proposed by Morgan identify prevailing *discourses* of English, by which I mean those systematic (although not entirely exclusive) ways in which English is thought, spoken, and written about that not only define but just as importantly also regulate notions of what subject English is and what it should and might become in a classroom. Morgan (1997) calls these various discourses of English aesthetic, ethical, rhetorical, and political. Ball, Kenny, and Gardiner (1990) delineate functional, cultural, progressive, and critical discourses of English. While equating categories can be somewhat misleading, it does seem reasonable to note that similar social and educational concerns prevail within the discursive groupings noted by these authors: rhetorical-functional, aesthetic-cultural, ethical-progressive, and political-critical. My intention here is not to provide extensive explanations of these discourses but only to point to their wide availability, their particular sediment in a geography of English, and their embodiment as partial "working knowledge" for beginning teachers of English.

The beginning teachers of English I encounter in secondary English studies stake out their initial pedagogical positions based on their varying degrees of knowledge of and investment in particular discourses. In other words, these discourses are already, in certain ways, part of their educational biographies, that series of previous experiences constituted around subject English. Early on in the course and prior to any discussion of the discourses mentioned above, their constitutive (discursive) frameworks are clear in numerous examples of how students initially name their positions and perspectives within English. For example, many students forge an argument for reclaiming what they see as a lost or lapsed focus within English on communication skills, by which they mean certain notions of appropriate usage, grammar, and modelled writing. Others bemoan impoverished imaginations malnourished by global popular culture and untuned to a sense of cultural heritage and the great literature that characterizes it. Still others beseech the importance of personal growth through student-centered reading and writing designed to explore individuality, promote self-esteem, and encourage social tolerance. And a few more have a strongly held suspicion that English has been "up to no good" for too long and see social and cultural criticism as an ethical project too long overlooked within an English notorious for its elitist texts, its intolerance of language difference, and its rampant individualism. It should be noted that students do not necessarily stake singular positions; instead, and often, many or all of these positions may be voiced at different times by the same student.

Even here, in these rudimentary sketches of partial positions, can be seen the compatibility and alignment among the previously outlined discourses named by Morgan (1997) and Ball et al. (1990): communication skills and rhetorical-functional discourses, cultural heritage and aesthetic-cultural discourses, personal growth and ethical-progressive discourses, and, finally, social and cultural criticism and political-critical discourses. Morgan (1997) and Ball et al. (1990) do point out, and it is clear to students, that these discursive categories are not tidy; seepage and overlap are not uncommon. But their delineation nonetheless focuses a crucial point: English is a construct, not a given or an essence; and the construct of English is not monolithic.

Faced with these competing versions of English, many beginning teachers are wary of recognizing their contradictory character. Rather, the inclination is to attempt to see value in all versions and to present an argument for their respective uses in varying contexts in English classrooms. This inclination should not be surprising. While contradiction is a fact of life, it is a rarely valued one. Contradictions are commonly viewed as weaknesses and should therefore be resolved or denied. Less often are contradictions viewed as productive, as unsettled spaces where irresolve might lead to new directions. Caught in a contradiction, one has the opportunity to change. Indeed, contradiction is the fertile seedbed of change.

At this point, in an effort to heighten their contradictions, I encourage students to examine how it is that an argument for a liberal smorgasbord of versions of English is an existing embodiment of unresolved historical contradictions which are part of their present story with and of English. Undoubtedly, contradiction is a common, even inevitable, characteristic of practice; but it is a productive characteristic only when it is examined, is heightened, and results in redefined practice. It is this process that allows an exploration of the ethical dilemma: What version(s) of English represent and provide space to accomplish important social, cultural, and educational objectives, and on what basis does one decide? Herein, then, students question not just how to teach communications skills. More pointedly, they question how best to explore pedagogically the need of students to function within an ethos of social expectations around communication while, simultaneously, they explore and savour issues of diversity, creativity, and cultural identity as they relate to language usage and expression.

Clarified for students by an examination of such struggles is another crucial and, perhaps, more disquieting point: Discourses of English shape not only a notion of the curriculum subject but also a world view, a view of ourselves and others, and, de facto, such views suggest ways of acting which are or are not in accordance with those views; that is, these discourses are regulatory. Competing versions of English are not innocent; nor are these competing versions only about personally different or preferred notions of practice, different ways of doing the same thing, or different means to the same end. These competing versions of English are just that: competing. They are different ways of doing *different* things, of participating in and (re)producing different versions of reality, different notions of social relationships, and different social dreams. In short, these competing versions of English are deeply political; they are about relations of power and the extent to which they are sanctioned, reiterated, and challenged through subject English.

Finally, these discourses, while they publicly circulate and are debated and valued in a plethora of ways, are fundamentally and ultimately within and of us. The struggles are already embodied. For this reason, an examination of these discourses is inevitably conflicted and painful. This process, after all, is about confronting the histories and implications of our beliefs and about alliances and affiliations—passionate contracts—formed without full or adequate disclosure, without access to "the fine print," the fuller implications of being "onside." This realization is part of a hard lesson in constitutive identity, in the habits of discourse and in the habitats habitual discourses build for us. This moment is a point at which to ponder the question of what it is one has become and the legacy of investment and desire that is the story of how it is one has become that which one may or may not wish to remain. Constituted within discourse, then, one is not oneself alone. Nor are the beliefs one holds merely one's own. And they may or may not be worthy of reproduction.

RECONSTITUTING ENGLISH

Given an opportunity to investigate the constitutive base of English and their biographical investments in it, beginning teachers of English gain insight into the macropolitics of practice, the embodied microtraces of these politics evidenced in personal biography, and the unsettling legacy of unexamined beliefs-in-practice. For these beginning teachers, practice as contradictory and contingent develops new meaning and becomes a new point of rigor for developing and examining their own evolving practices as they prepare for beginning teaching. But what happens to such (dis)positions upon beginning teaching?

The dominant structure of teacher education is such that the maintenance of the status quo within teaching is more often ensured than challenged. The trajectory into which beginning teachers of English are placed and to which I referred at the beginning of this chapter—competing versions of English presented by curriculum guides, professional teachers, and secondary English studies courses—presents a complex and competitive navigational field. If beginning teachers have not had an opportunity to develop within teacher education the understandings necessary to negotiate this contradictory field, the understandable inclination often is to suspend the conviction of one's own evolving beliefs as they might translate into contingent practice. Without certain kinds of support or understanding from schools, for beginning teachers, it can seem easier to ride the normative wave of what is on offer in a specific placement with a supervising (or cooperating) professional teacher with whom a beginning teacher is assigned during beginning teaching.

This strategy of maneuverance—*splitting off*—allows the beginning teacher to cope within the immediate (and threatening) context, seeing any prior commitment to alternative practices as "on hold" rather than forsaken. In such a scenario, regardless of what versions of English are held by either the beginning or professional teacher, splitting off, while widely advocated as a "survival strategy" for beginning teachers, is deeply problematic. What splitting off can accomplish for the beginning teacher of English is a denial of agency and a refusal of the very human capacity to effect change where change is necessary. Furthermore, what splitting off encapsulates is a hegemonic moment when the political force field of education comes to (w)rest on bodies of promise and hope.

In this scenario, not only is an educational opportunity compromised or lost, but the beginning teacher learns the powerful lesson that the given is not easily disputed or disrupted. This conclusion seems reasonable for, if there is a time when dreams of the possible might be shaped and practiced, should that time not be when one has the opportunity to access various strong institutional supports, in theory, the university and the schools? Undoubtedly, certain kinds of support do exist for beginning teachers, but its face is usually a technicist one in order to cover the "3-m" concerns of method, management, and morale; from a normative perspective of teaching, this support is believed to be the most necessary kind. Effectively sidelined by such foci, however, is a concern for what education is about and how its normative preoccupations and daily enactments, to the exclusion of other concerns, can be obstacles to visions and versions of change.

Such an experience is jarring for beginning English teachers who are learning to ponder their educational investments and their previously held views of English and who are asking the very central question of how they want their relationships to (or knowledge to) look while they also speculate on practices in keeping with these questions. There is a historic dissatisfaction among students of teacher education programs, but much of the dissatisfaction is centered around what is not learned in these programs in relation to the normative, technicist (often called "practical") work of teaching. Clearly, this divide between program and practice is not impossible as, perennially, beginning teachers become professional teachers and successfully bridge this perceived gap. But dissatisfaction with teacher education programs is different from dissatisfaction with teaching. What of those who have come to understand how desire runs through learning, how knowledge is vested, and how identity is shaped and reshaped within the culture of classrooms? Without support to become the teachers they are learning they want to be, these beginning teachers of English may learn that there is little space in which to negotiate the differences such insights accrue for the classroom. In this lesson, desire begets vexation, and vexation erodes hope and curtains the spirit. No number of exciting new techniques for maintaining the very old status quo are of solace here.

CONCLUSION

To move beyond romanticized notions of English is often to retreat from and to reconfigure once familiar and highly invested desires embedded in our personal and social histories. Such letting go can be difficult, even while also hopeful and expansive. But, *how* is it possible to create a context where such discursive movement is possible and not merely desirous? Where changing relationships to knowledge is not lamentable but given? Where dreams are not dismissable and hope does not dissolve into cynicism? Where dreams of the possible do not become dreams impossible to live (with)?

Merely to name the complexities and contradictions of educational investment in the context of competing expectations is not to create educational change. Naming alone can all too often result only in chaos, misgiving, and despair. But this caveat should not be construed as an argument for silence. Refusing to acknowledge ideological constraints and contradictions is not a reasonable educational alternative, even if it is a much-practiced one. Recognizing the limits of naming alone, though, does shore up the need to reconceptualize what is done within teacher education. Part of this reconceptualization would provide a central focus for beginning teachers to come to terms with the pretences of the scripts they embody and those that surround them. Such a focus would enable a space in which to design practices that, while contingent, are reflective and farsighted, forged out of a reshaped ethic of teaching, a working knowledge of the available, and a renewed desire for the possible.

Within such a reconceptualization, teacher educators would need not only to acknowledge the complex negotiation of contradictory and conflicting demands that are so heightened in beginning teaching but also to work constructively with students within this myriad of competing demands. This challenge requires rethinking pharmaceutical notions of curriculum practice courses as dispensaries of received and settled knowledge of how to proceed pedagogically within a subject area. Instead, such courses might be redesigned as sites on which the already formulated and sedimented is unsettled, where old relationships to knowledge are examined, and where the pedagogical premises of new relationships are forged. Such work is only possible if a teacher educator has a broad picture of the competing frameworks of a subject—in this case, English—a sense of the place of teacher biography and professional ethos in the actual navigation of these frameworks, and a vision of and a faith in the educationally possible.

Finally, the place of beginning teaching within a teacher education program, in its dominant forms, must also be rethought. Supervising (cooperating) teachers are commonly chosen based on their availability and not on their capacity as mentors who can work with beginning teachers over sustained periods around crucial issues of teacher education. Where this remains the case, it is unlikely that beginning teaching can be anything more than initiation into an already defined "club" into which one becomes acculturated and in which one learns the already established rules by which one will, ultimately, be governed. From this perspective, initiation can be fatalistic and claustrophobic; it is most certainly a perspective antithetical to reflection, to change, and indeed to education. Teacher education based on exploration, experimentation, and critical inquiry cannot flourish in such compromised circumstances—nor can the well-informed dreams of beginning teachers.

REFERENCES

Ball, S., Kenny, A., & Gardiner, D. (1990). Literacy, politics and the teaching of English. In I. Goodson & P. Medway (Eds.), *Bringing English to order* (pp. 47–86). London: Falmer Press.

Britzman, D. (1998). Some observations on the work of learning. *Journal of Curriculum Theorizing, 14*(2), 53–59.

Kelly, U. (1993a). *Marketing place: Cultural politics, regionalism and reading.* Halifax, NS: Fernwood Books.

Kelly, U. (1993b). Teaching English: Who's subject to what? In S. B. Straw & D. Bogdan (Eds.), *Constructive reading: Teaching beyond communication* (pp. 205–213). Portsmouth, NH: Boynton/Cook.

Kelly, U. (1997). *Schooling desire: Literacy, cultural politics and pedagogy.* New York: Routledge.

Morgan, W. (1997). *Critical literacy in the classroom: The art of the possible.* London: Routledge.

CHAPTER 5

"Words Is Changin' Every Day": Language and Literacy in the Urban Contact Zone

MARYANN DICKAR
New York University

The title of this chapter comes from an interview with a male high school student about his views on language. Asked his opinion of the Ebonics controversy very much in the news at the time he responded:

> Words is changin' every day. . . . Most people who listen to Rap they can't understand it. I am Hip-Hop. I used to be into Reggae stuff. Now, Ebonics is changin' every day. New words, I made up words, people made up words. I bring new words to people they didn't even know about. Ebonics, it's just people's little code, it's a whole 'nother language, yeah, but don't make that a class. You can't because it changes every day.[1]

A speaker powerfully asserting ownership. His language, dynamic— "changin' every day." In contrast, other languages, like Standard English, are more fixed, lacking this vibrant quality. The very term *standard* implies rules, fixed and predictable. Here hip-hop is central to his sense of language; it is a source of new expressions as well as a means for disseminating the new language. Ebonics, for him, is spontaneous and improvisational because it is of the moment, constantly changing to meet new discursive needs. And it is democratic: Anyone can participate in the creation of words. He makes up words; others make up words. His statement compels because he equates Ebonics with distinctly Black forms of expression, like hip-hop and reggae, and connects it to a broader Black culture. Lastly, I am struck by the tone. This student cherishes the language he speaks. He is proud of it as an expression of his identity. As he said, "I am hip hop." He is his language.

This quote highlights a fundamental crisis facing urban schools: Language and identity are intertwined and resistance to standard language forms equals resistance to the denigration of Black identity and culture. English educators must grapple with this crisis. What is our role in promoting Standard English and how do we address students who see much of the school's efforts including its language policies as attacks on their culture? How do the linguistic choices students make inform their academic achievement and their relationship to schooling? What is at stake in the tension between local languages and Standard English?

I explored these questions by asking 35 inner-city students how they saw Standard English and how they employed code switching, the practice of changing dialects (or codes) in different contexts, both in and out of the classroom. The students were split over the ways they should use language in school. Some felt that using Standard English was dishonest, a violation of the self, while others perceived the ability to code-switch as a crucial skill to future success. Their differing perceptions of language are informed by their varying notions of Blackness, senses of group solidarity, and relationships to the dominant culture, particularly ideas about individualism and assimilation.

Though there was no consensus about language use in school, students generally agreed there were some clear rules. Most felt it was inappropriate to speak Ebonics in formal settings like the job interview. They also generally agreed that it was okay to speak Ebonics in the halls and the street. However, when asked if they should be expected to speak Standard English in the classroom, the responses divided into three equal camps: those who opposed the imposition of Standard English in the classroom, those who felt that the school should impose Standard English, and those not sure or not stating an opinion. Student responses to these issues reveal the complexity of the politics of language and also how contested the classroom is. It is apparently a space controlled and defined by teachers and the dominant society while also being terrain for student expression and resistance. Significantly, students who felt Standard English should be required in classrooms were three times more likely to graduate from high school than students who supported the use of local languages. Student positions on language were deeply connected to perceptions of culture, community, and the meaning or value of schooling.

My interviews were conducted at a comprehensive public high school in New York City, where I had taught from 1996–2000.[2] This school serves an overwhelmingly Black[3] population (96% Black and 4% Hispanic) with the majority being immigrants or children of immigrants from the Caribbean. Three quarters of the students lived in poverty as indicated by their lunch forms. Although this school had some of the lowest test scores and highest dropout rates in New York City, it was also undergoing progressive school reform that included more democratic governance and classroom practices. I found that language policy was a site of cultural struggle between students and school personnel—a contact zone.

CONTACT ZONES AND URBAN SCHOOLS

Mary Louise Pratt (1991) defines *contact zones* as "social spaces where cultures meet, clash, and grapple with each other, often in contexts of highly asymmetrical relations of power, such as colonialism, slavery, or their aftermaths as they are lived out in many parts of the world today" (p. 34). Contact zones are not places where two cultures meet on equal or equivalent terms; rather, such zones are specifically places of domination, cross-purposes, competing agendas, and resistance. Inner-city schools are such conflicted places. They are institutions formally controlled and designed by the state with an official mandate of social reproduction. Students enter these institutions with values inculcated in their homes and communities as well as with identities that may be oppositional to the dominant norm. They are confronted with a whole system of expectations and behaviors to which they must adjust. The entry rituals employed by many inner-city high schools provide a dramatic illustration.

When students arrive at school in the morning, they are greeted by the institution with security screening. Students walk through full-body metal detectors, and their bags are x-rayed much like entering an airport. If they trigger an alarm, they may be sent to another station for more aggressive scanning, a second full-body scan, and a search with handheld scanners. Their bags and pockets may be gone through as well.

The purpose of scanning is ostensibly safety, to keep weapons out of the school, but all kinds of contraband are removed from student bodies—anything that could be used as a weapon, including scissors or long hairpins. Students are also searched for banned items such as portable stereos, beepers, cell phones, magic markers, highlighters, whiteout, cigarettes, lighters, matches, drugs, and anything associated with gangs, like bandannas or beads. These searches are often tense and marked with hostility between students and the guards who conduct them. Not only are students further searched if they make the alarm go off, but students are also randomly sent for further screening if a guard even thinks they look suspicious.

Many students accepted scanning as a safety measure, but expressed anger as well:

When you come to school . . . they give you rules, "No walkmans, no hats, no beepers or pagers, no telephones." But, still students bring it, so I think that scanning is good because . . . when students do bring their stuff to school, they take it away. . . . But, in a way, to contradict myself, um, scanning makes you feel like you're in prison because you can't go out of the school and you see bars all over the place—what else are you to think, that you're in some kind of jail. And they're sitting there scanning you and they want to scale up on you and take all your stuff and go through your hair and stuff like that. . . . Like if you have a scarf on . . . they be all up in your scarf with the scanning thing.

Another student explained more about scanning procedures:

When you come in in the morning, and you wearing Timbs and your baggy jeans. . . . you got the doo-rag on, your jacket unzipped and you got your hat on, whatever, and you come through the machine and you beep, automatically they gonna send you around through the whole phase. And then, like for me, for instance, I come here with my shoes, my slacks and I dress my preppy prep and I come through and the thing beeps, they don't send me around. They just like, you could go upstairs. They figure, ah look at the way he dress, he not gonna kill nobody. Like that.

Though scanning is accepted by most students because of safety, they also suggest that something more than the removal of weapons is going on. At the moment when students meet the school, the institution establishes its dominance physically and symbolically through its security apparatus. Though students offer resistance through verbal complaints, impatient gestures, hostile body postures, and even some scuffles during scanning, this is a visceral and violent ritual demonstrating who has power and who does not. Importantly, what interviewed students complained about was not the removal of banned items, but rather that specific forms of dress associated with Blacks and Black youth culture are singled out for additional scrutiny like head wraps, baggy pants, and doo-rags. These students perceive that Black cultural identity is attacked during scanning, which sets the tone for student distrust.

As a method of control, scanning can be viewed as the *weapons of the strong*, a term anthropologist James Scott (1990) uses to denote regulation adopted by groups in power, in contrast to the *weapons of the weak*, everyday forms of resistance of relatively powerless groups. "Weak" weapons include both the quiet and not-so-quiet sabotage of school efforts through actions such as absenteeism, cutting classes, wasting time in class, and class disruptions through which students undermine the school's efforts. Thus, at the schoolhouse door where scanning apparatus awaits sleepy students first thing in the morning, the lines are drawn.

Scanning is an example of how schools are contact zones of asymmetrical power where cultures do not meet in benign or friendly encounters, but rather where subordinate groups confront the institutions that dominate them. I do not wish to suggest, however, that schools are completely controlling and oppressive institutions. Though they are these things, they are also social and communal places where multiple purposes clash. The ambiguity around what idiom should reign in the classroom suggests that classrooms, like scanning, are places where cultures meet and where power is negotiated.

THE CASE FOR BLACK VERNACULAR ENGLISH IN THE CLASSROOM

To many students, Ebonics or Black Vernacular English (BVE) is the language of Black people, and Standard English is the language of White people. One student made the connection outright: "If you speak perfect English, they'll say, 'what are you, White?'" Loyalty to a peer and race group was judged through language use, so students faced significant peer pressure to reject the language of White people.

Scholars of African American language have noted the construction of Standard English as "White" English. Geneval Smitherman (1977/1986) acknowledges this:

> Historically, Black speech has been demanded of those who wish to retain close affinities with the Black community, and intrusions of White English are likely to be frowned upon and any Black users thereof promptly ostracized by the group. Talkin proper (trying to sound White) just ain't considered cool. On the other hand, White America has insisted upon White English as the price of admission into its economic and social mainstream. (p. 12)

The students interviewed were well aware of these conflicting demands, and proponents of Black Vernacular English saw speaking the language of White America as a betrayal of the Black peer group.

The construction of Standard English as a White language was central to the critique made by student proponents of BVE. One male student described the imposition of Standard English as a project of White domination. "White language, you got the state of mind. They enslaved your brain." Other students elaborated on the ways the imposition of Standard English derided their group identity. John offered a broad critique of the imposition of Standard English:

Do you use different language than when you're in class?

Yeah it's like you're two totally different people, but not with everybody. Like, cause, one way, when you in the hallway with your friends, you speak, basically you speak in Ebonics, like that and you talkin' slang with your friends and they understand what you sayin'. And then when you in the classroom, you know you can't say, "Nah, nah, know what I mean, word up, and whatever," the teacher don't really be understandin' you, so you got to like, well, okay, "You see this is the problem I have" and stuff like that.

Do students tend to drop the slang when they come into the room?

Me, I don't drop the slang when I'm in the classroom. That's how I talk and that's the way I write. Cause I know, cause most of the time I know if I change, if I write the way that they want me to write, they gonna be like, you didn't write this. You a totally different person, somebody else wrote this for you. So, I don't even waste my time.

If you write in Standard English, teachers will think you copied it from somewhere?

Yeah, I think it's one. Cause they don't, I think its they think you can't speak Standard English. And me, I really see that there's no point in this cause instead of somebody sayin' it in Standard English, "Well, how are you doin' today?" "Oh, I'm doing fine, everything is good." And they tell you, "how's the kids?" And like with me, I could say that all in one, all in one movement. Like, when I see [names a friend], I be like, I could either say, "What up?" and he be like, "Nothin" so I know everything is good, or I could just give him a pound [gesture] and we just said everything that they said in a pound! And I know like if I go to give him a pound and he doesn't give me a pound, then I know there's something wrong. So that way, I don't have to say, "Well, what's wrong?" when we go through that whole conversation. Like that. It's a whole lot quicker then just doin' Standard English.

Do you think you need to know Standard English?

I don't think, well, I think you do need to know Standard English cause you want to get into situations where that's the only way you gonna get out. But mainly, and it also depends on where you live. Like where I live and like where [his friend] lives, you don't have no use for Standard English. It doesn't really, nobody really cares if you speak Standard English or not.

John's discussion of his language use addresses the key points that other proponents of BVE raised as well. First, he felt that school required him to be two different people, his real self in the hall and someone else in the classroom. A hundred years ago, W. E. B. DuBois (1903/1986) discussed "double-consciousness"—the pain caused by the "two-ness" of being African American and of being American while wishing to be one, whole, undivided person (p. 364). Here, John refused to split himself by refusing to speak Standard English. Using Standard English instead of Ebonics creates a double bind. On the one hand, it is not the language he prefers, and on the other, he suspects, the teachers will not accept such work because they think he cannot use Standard English effectively. His sense that the teachers wouldn't believe he wrote in Standard English anyway also suggests the great suspicion students hold toward the school. Finally, he prefers Ebonics because it is so much more efficient in his circle. He includes as part of his language a "pound," or gesture. He imitates an overly formal and polite conversation to point out how much must be said to achieve the information shared in a single gesture. Thus Standard English in his eyes turns out to be inefficient.

These themes of wholeness, authenticity, and efficiency emerged in several interviews. As Florence asserted, "You should be yourself." Derek felt, "They should speak the way how they speak, they shouldn't change for nobody." Students who defended their vernacular language as part of their culture also echoed this sense, that though Standard English was important, language reflected a core part of a person's identity and had to be respected. In explaining her decision to only speak Ebonics, Tina said, "Like I gotta just be myself, if I can't be myself, you know, what's the use of being here." For these students, code switching was part of "double-consciousness" and was a violation of the self.

THE CASE FOR STANDARD ENGLISH—
WHAT OF THE THIRD WHO SUPPORTED IT?

Students who supported the use of Standard English in the classroom rejected the construction of Blackness promoted by Ebonics supporters. They sought to separate Blackness from BVE to open up avenues for themselves in which they could be middle-class, successful, and Black. They also created a hierarchy that valued Standard English as the language of success, intelligence, and adulthood. Students who supported Standard English were more likely to identify with school and academic success and diminish BVE as a language of low aspirations and lower-class positions in the present and the future. For them, the use of Standard English was a tool for upward mobility, not an assault on Black identity.

Leroy, who promoted Standard English, was critical of Ebonics because it reinforced racist stereotypes of Black people. His critique is instructive because although advocates of Ebonics often constructed speakers of Standard English as traitors and occasionally as "White," those who preferred Standard English were often equally motivated by group solidarity:

They talk "ghetto," not Black. Like, "is," "ain't no nigga," "ain't got that son," "illin'," "chillin'," "buggin'," "what is you doin'." People think that Black people talk like the students in this school. But they don't—that is ghetto! Ebonics is crap! It's ghetto. People think Black people can't speak better. . . . It's that White people perceive that that's how all Black people speak. That's how ghetto people speak. To your friends, you can talk any way, but you have to know the boundaries.

Leroy criticized the use of Ebonics in public settings because he feared it defined Black people negatively. Importantly, though his peers identified Ebonics with Black identity, he specifically separated it, identifying the language widely used by students as "ghetto," not Black. By separating negative attributes like lack of education and poverty as ghetto, he preserved a positive Black identity that transcended these stereotypes.

The separation of ghetto from Black, is a class-based division. Such a division may be a defensive response against those who define academically successful students as White. Once in a class I was teaching, a student accused Leroy and a few others of being White because they owned computers and were good students. When I asked him to interpret this event for me, he said the remark was more aimed at the economic class of high achievers. Then he offered a class-based analysis of the animosity between serious academic students and those who attack them for breaking solidarity with their race:

They just most of the times, you know, they're like offended, no, they're mad at you because you have a better upbringing you know. You're more fortunate than they are. You have like a house instead of an apartment and stuff like that. . . . Most of the time, you know, it's like kids who have like a secure financial place for them to live in or whatever, usually those students do better you know, that's a fact. Not that it's necessary, you know, you must have a house or a computer, or whatever, but for the most part if you have a secure home, a mother and a father, for the most part, these are the kids that do well.

Leroy saw academic success and failure as products of socioeconomic class. As in his discussion of Ebonics, he tried to separate Black identity from lower class status. Whereas the other student had equated middle-class tropes, such as computer ownership, with Whiteness, Leroy rejects this equation; instead, such things are middle-class, not White, benefits. By separating Black identity from a subordinate class position, he promotes a competing notion of Blackness that allows him to pursue academic and middle-class goals without compromising Black identity.

Leroy's support for Standard English ties into his perception that low-class status is wrongly affixed to Black identity. "White people think that's how all Black people speak. That's how ghetto people speak." The role of language connects directly to the core of identity. Separating Ebonics from Black identity frees Black identity from marginalization. Signithia Fordham (1996) has pointed out that African American students often construct academic success as "White" and refuse to strive for it because such actions are perceived as an assault on Blackness. Success in school requires submission and buying into dominant values that often negatively construct Blackness. Many students resist White domination by rejecting academic success. However, she argues that high-achieving African American students are often resisting these very same negative constructions of Blackness by challenging racist stereotypes. The students I studied who felt strongly about the use of Standard English were generally high-achieving or aspired to be, demonstrating the kind of resistance Fordham found in her study on African American high school students and academic success.

A number of proponents of Standard English supported separating Black identity from specific linguistic and class tropes. Another advocate of Standard English, Lakisha, attacked Ebonics because it keeps her race down.

> It is very important because the students, in this world, you cannot use Ebonics to speak to your should be or might be boss. You have to speak proper English, cause that's what we were taught when we came to America. I mean, we don't speak African or Latin, you know, Spanish, we speak English. . . . Ebonics, I feel, is just a trick to make, most people, you know people can't get a job with that language. So when it's taught to people who already don't know how to speak better, you know, then they gonna go into the world not knowing how to speak proper at all and people are not going to understand you. You're not gonna get anywhere, pretty much.

Though Lakisha may have interpreted the Ebonics debate to mean the teaching of BVE in place of Standard English, she identified the widespread use of Ebonics and the lack of knowledge of Standard English as detrimental to the upward mobility of Black people. As Tashona said, "If you want to excel in life, you have to speak Standard English."

Class-inflected understandings of race and language permeated much of the support for teaching Standard English and using it in the classroom. Some students felt that some of their peers—and sometimes they themselves—could not effectively switch to Standard English. This inability was perceived negatively. Lakisha links the use of BVE to lower class status by pointing to the family as having failed to teach Standard English:

A lot of them still speak the slang, they don't learn any better, even at home. Some of the parents now, they don't know better themselves. They teach their kids what they know and the kids come in the school not knowing any better but carrying what they know from home to school. But, you know, I for instance, I know better.

Insisting that she does know better, Lakisha defines herself as superior to those who don't. Like Leroy who was sensitive to class, she too creates a division based on upbringing and aspirations.

Rovell Solomon (1992) points out that the school is the key to upward mobility for West Indians. For many Caribbean students, immigration to America offers educational opportunities denied them in their home countries. Proponents of Standard English hoped that the school would deliver the educational goods they need to move up economically. Lisa Delpit (1995) has argued that by not teaching minority and marginalized children the dominant language, the school is withholding crucial tools for future advancement and survival. These students, too, echo her demand that the school help them develop the cultural capital they will need to compete in a market that will often be hostile to them.

Though proponents of Standard English identified positively with being Black, their critiques of Ebonics echoed racist attacks on Black culture in subtle ways. Students constantly placed Standard English and Ebonics in hierarchies that almost always favored Standard English. As Tashona explained,

Well, I speak differently around my peers than I do in front of adults. So, I want to be perceived as an intelligent intellectual, so I'll speak with dignity and I'll speak with pride and I speak with some intelligence. I know something. So that they'll know that.

Standard English is represented here as the language of intelligence, pride, and dignity. By implication, Ebonics does not convey these qualities. In addition, many students perceived Ebonics as a language for children, but not for adults, establishing another unbalanced hierarchy. Tameeka reiterated that students should use Standard English in the classroom because "you're talking to an adult, which is the teacher, talk on an adult level."

In short, much of the tension surrounding Ebonics lies in its problematic status as a language—Is it a language or a colloquial slang? Though many students felt it wasn't to be spoken around adults, many adults speak it, and some students perceived that many adults did not know Standard English. Thus, although it is not simply youth slang, it often is construed as such, which therefore renders it less legitimate than the language of adults, Standard English.

Such are the conflicts and contradictions of unequal power relations in a contact zone.

CLASSROOMS AS CONTACT ZONES

These contrasting perspectives on the language of the classroom show us that though school authority exhibits an aggressive profile at the borders—the entry rituals around scanning—inside the building there are many spaces—the cafeteria, the halls, the classroom—where power relations vary in profile. In the halls, where student language is the dominant idiom, power tilts in the students' favor thus enabling the deepest articulation of student culture. As power shifts, so too do opportunities for student expression. The classroom is ambiguous—teachers compete for authority with student discourse and no clear regime dominates. Despite the authority granted the teacher as institutional representative of school and society, there is much student resistance. Language as a site of struggle and as a contact zone comes to the fore in the classroom because education is a social experience mediated by verbal and textual discourse.

Most students acknowledged that the classroom is polyglot, that no single idiom prevailed. However, the teachers speak in Standard English, and the texts students read are in Standard English. Students are expected to use Standard English in their written work and were judged accordingly. Teachers at this urban school also were conflicted about the language policies they imposed. Most teachers interviewed (17 teachers were) did not correct student speech for the most part, recognizing that language is linked to culture and to embarrass a student openly is to diminish the student and his or her culture. However, most teachers more readily corrected written work though even here the tendency was to focus on the most severe grammatical errors. Other teachers focused more on content than form. The variation among teachers, vis à vis linguistic expectations and correction, highlights how uncertain all participants were about the status of the classroom as either student or teacher space.

CONCLUSIONS

School records showed that those students who identified with BVE were far less likely to be making academic progress. Of the 11 students who supported the use of Ebonics in the classroom, only 4 graduated in 4 years and most of the others did not graduate at all. On the other hand, all but one of the 12 students who supported the use of Standard English graduated high school in 4 years.

This suggests that student perceptions of language connect to a general disposition toward schooling and that those who reject the language of broader communication often resist many other aspects of schooling as well.

The complexities of the language issue mean that many English teachers working in city schools end up in a contradictory place: They are part of the institution that scans head wraps for weapons, yet at the same time can exercise some autonomy in the classroom. Teachers are border workers in the sense that they are part of the educational apparatus but also have significant contact with students. Unlike the impersonal interactions experienced by students during scanning, classroom interactions are far more personal and contextual. The contested nature of language in the classroom is just one example of how the classroom operates as a contact zone and presents English teachers with unique and important challenges.

How do we resolve these tensions around language presented by the students interviewed? How do we respect the concerns of students who reject Standard English while also increasing their fluency and confidence in Standard English and perhaps also their possibility of graduating? How can the English language arts classroom be a place to encourage student self-expression while also empowering students, both in the language they bring with them and in Standard English?

Because language is about power, students need to become conscious of the ways they might control language. Moving explicitly in the direction of critical pedagogy, the English language arts classroom might be a place where text is drawn from social context. Teachers can help students engage ethnographies, oral histories, and life struggles faced in their communities each day. Given real-life contexts to write about can help them find their voices in Standard English because they will also find their audience. The work of the Foxfire network, where students write the history of their community for publication (McDonald, 1992), provides one powerful example. Through such activities English teachers can immerse students in a literate culture of their own making.

The English classroom is also a place that can easily represent student experience through existing rich literary traditions. The growth in popularity of poetry slam teams and the general popularity of poetry among many inner-city students is another place to create meaningful connections between students and schooling. Developing a curriculum around popular forms of expression offers opportunities to value the incredible linguistic skills many students bring into the classroom, which all too often remain untapped. Through such interventions, English classrooms can be spaces in which the domination of the institution can be subverted and where students can be whole, authentic, and heard.

NOTES

1. Admittedly, he thought the Ebonics curriculum was aimed at teaching students Black Vernacular English or what most students referred to as slang, though the intention of the curriculum was to teach Standard English while valuing local languages as well. Because these interviews took place during the hotly contested Ebonics controversy, Ebonics was used to refer to Black Vernacular English (BVE), and I will use these terms interchangeably throughout the rest of the chapter.

2. These interviews were part of a larger study that included interviews with 42 students and 17 teachers as well as extensive observation at the school. Each participant was interviewed for between 30 and 90 minutes. All names included in this essay are pseudonyms.

3. I use the term Black to describe students because they were from many Caribbean and African countries as well as different parts of the United States, making terms like African American too narrow. Also, many students identified themselves as Black but not as African American.

REFERENCES

Delpit, L. (1995). The silenced dialogue: Power and pedagogy in educating other people's children. *Other people's children: Cultural conflict in the classroom*. New York: New Press.

DuBois, W. E. B. (1986). Of our spiritual strivings. *The Souls of Black Folk*. In *W. E. B. DuBois writings*. New York: Library of America. (Original work published 1903)

Fordham, S. (1996). *Blacked out: Dilemmas of race, identity, and success at Capital High*. Chicago: University of Chicago Press.

McDonald, J. (1992). *Teaching: Making sense of an uncertain craft*. New York: Teachers College Press.

Pratt, M. L. (1991). Arts of the contact zone. *Profession 91* (pp. 33–40). New York: Modern Language Association.

Scott, J. C. (1990). *Domination and the arts of resistance: Hidden transcripts*. New Haven, CT: Yale University Press.

Smitherman, G. (1986). *Talkin and testifyin: The language of Black America*. Detroit, MI: Wayne State University Press. (Original work published 1977)

Solomon, R. P. (1992). *Black resistance in high school: Forging a separatist culture*. Albany: State University of New York Press.

CHAPTER 6

Tightrope Walkers: The Balancing and Unbalancing Act of Teaching Writing

Jill Kedersha McClay
University of Alberta

> *Rigidly*
> *I pose on a platform.*
> *Balancing,*
> *Pole in hand.*
> *Waiting,*
> *Barely breathing.*
> —Joyce MacDonald

This first stanza of Joyce MacDonald's poem, "Tightrope Walking," establishes the metaphor for her attempts to achieve balance as a teacher who must "perform" to the expectant crowd. Joyce, like all teachers, learns to teach in a public arena, as a performance, before an audience who, she fears, may await the spectacle of her fall as eagerly as that of her successful navigation of the tightrope.

Like many other beginning as well as experienced English language arts teachers, Joyce participates in a writers' workshop. She shares her writing in draft and as a finished product, provides writing conference support for peers, and explores the nature of her own writing processes, while simultaneously exploring what it means to be a teacher of writing. From my work with beginning teachers and adolescents in writers' workshops, and from ongoing research in writing theory and pedagogy, I have come to think of teaching writing as a balancing act. In our teaching, we often strive for equilibrium, but in teaching writing (and perhaps in all teaching), equilibrium is a momentary suspension of opposing forces, an intake of breath before one force unbalances us and we compensate toward the opposite. As we gain experience and expertise, our swings to adjust the balance become smaller, but still we sway and tip moment by moment.

THE BALANCE OF TEACHING AND LEARNING

The difficult process of learning to teach involves negotiation and realignment of one's self-image, as a beginning teacher assumes the role of teacher while still feeling very much a student. Indeed, teachers are accustomed to thinking of themselves as "lifelong learners," to use the tired jargon of human resources officers. But when beginning teachers long for that impression of personal security and poise that they sensed in their best teachers, the role of "lifelong learner" can seem frustrating and dangerous. There is sometimes a rush toward certainty in teaching.

For an English language arts teacher, the process of developing confidence is additionally complicated by the nature of the discipline and by the current orthodoxy advocated for the teaching of writing. As teachers develop generic "teacher identities," we also negotiate our relationships with our chosen discipline. What does it mean to see myself as a teacher of English language arts? What does it mean for me to be a teacher of writing?

English language arts as a school subject has been both applauded and condemned as virtually a "contentless" subject. There is not an obvious body of knowledge to be mastered or arranged sequentially. Many English language arts teachers consider the broad focus on language development and language for learning to be a primary attraction of English language arts: It is a limitless domain of possibilities. The expansive ambiguity of the subject allows teachers to focus upon students' language development and encourages process orientations to teaching. However, given the current reality of pressure for "accountability" in the guise of ever-higher scores on standardized external examinations, it is no wonder that teachers, particularly beginning teachers, may view the ambiguity and breadth of English language arts as a liability rather than as a strength.

Nevertheless, contemporary research and practice extol the benefits of process approaches to the teaching of writing. Leading English educators encourage teachers of writing to explore the process of writing with their students: Teachers of writing ought to be writers themselves. From the foundational work of such researchers and teachers as Britton et al. (1975), Graves (1985), Murray (1985), Atwell (1987), and Romano (1987), among others, leadership in the English education community has developed a conception of the teacher-as-writer and of process approaches to teach writing "from the inside out" (Kirby, Liner, & Vinz, 1988). Teachers are encouraged to consider themselves as writers who "live between the lines" (Calkins, 1991) and who model such a writerly life for their students, creating a celebratory writing community in their classrooms.

Such celebratory writing communities can foster powerful experiential learning about writing and teaching. Teacher educators have taken the maxim "we teach as we were taught" as an imperative to provide experiential learning in order to give preservice teachers a grounding of productive experience in teaching methods that may be unfamiliar to them. Often this means that we introduce new teachers to conceptions of English language arts that are outside the realm of their school experiences, experiences which initially encouraged their interest in selecting English language arts as a primary area of study. Many beginning English language arts teachers thus shoulder a double task in "composing a teaching life" (Vinz, 1993): simultaneously to compose themselves as teachers and to compose themselves as writers. Teachers need to develop their voices in teaching as well as in writing in order to help children develop *their* voices in writing. (All of this is accomplished, of course, with administrators, parents, readers of standardized test scores—not to mention their own "inner Puritans" who strive for excellence—looking over their shoulders! It's no wonder that stress is a leading cause of teacher burnout in the early years.)

Working to establish a productive, safe writing workshop environment with beginning teachers, I know that many core issues of teaching writing will surface, sometimes painfully. The following few examples from a writers' workshop among beginning teachers illustrate such learning.

While many students participating in a writers' workshop discover the benefits of peer conferences and of talking with others to help clarify their own intentions in writing, Angela also learned about the negative potential of peer conferences:

> The problems started to occur . . . when I asked for my first peer conference. I came to the realization that everyone seems to have a wish to be a writer. My self-confidence fell to an all-time low while a peer started to rewrite my [poem], notwithstanding the fact that the purpose of the peer conference was specifically to edit for humor. It probably wouldn't have been so bad if he had polished the writing as well, so that I wouldn't have had to try to work with it. I discovered that it is virtually impossible to continue editing after it has evolved into someone else's work. . . . I decided to go back to my *own* work and continue with it.

By extension, Angela understood clearly that if peers can so easily appropriate ownership, how much more easily teachers can do so. She learned to retain ownership of her writing despite the pressures of well-meaning peers;

more important, she realized her own potential as a teacher to appropriate ownership unintentionally.

Cara learned about the connection between publication for real audiences and attention to details of proofreading when she wrote a letter to the editor of her local paper. The possibility of actual publication made her serious about proofreading and editing conferences. For the first time, she sought another proofreader for her work: "I shopped around for someone with good grammar skills." After days of anxiously flipping to the letters page of the newspaper, she found her letter printed. "When it finally was printed, I told everyone and I cut it out and put it on the fridge. Through this I learned that recognition is a very important part of the writing process." Cara begins her teaching career with a keen interest in pursuing avenues of publication for her students.

Dave, father of a lively, affectionate toddler, struggled to write about his son. The first successful piece of writing that Dave composed about his son came as a result of a writing conference when I suggested that he not try to write about the extent of his love directly, but "just choose a moment." His poem captures a wry father-son moment and suggests the enormity of love in this father-and-son bond. It also provides Dave with a sense of how to help his future students write from their lives when they choose to do so.

The most important learning about writing that these beginning teachers can achieve is to trust their own learning to influence their teaching. Such confidence in the power of their own writing replaces or at least reduces their reliance upon mind-numbing writing exercises of the "descriptive paragraph" variety. It teaches them the power of writing—a power we can only learn by experiencing it. In this context, the quality of their writing is not as important as the struggle to express and craft ideas of importance.

THE UNBALANCE OF RISK-TAKING AND AUTHORITY

When a writers' workshop is conducted only among preservice teachers, the obvious question, "But will it work with kids?" will underpin all of our work. Writers often appreciate the structures, emphasis, and procedures of the workshop for their own development as writers, but doubt whether such structures, emphasis, and procedures will "work" with children of whatever age they happen to be preparing to teach. (Ironically, I usually find that some teachers assume that workshop approaches are beneficial for adults and for students of a *different* age—either older or younger—than the ones they are preparing to teach. When I work with elementary and secondary teachers together, we can unpack the assumptions of this myth nicely.) When these writers and beginning teachers also write with children, the learning is more powerful. The balancing act of teacher-learner, teacher-as-fellow-writer, and teacher-as-evaluator is a more intense, more consequential, and more risk-laden enterprise when teachers act as writers and teachers simultaneously. In an ongoing study of the developing practices of English language arts teachers in their "formative" years (loosely defined as years 2–7 of teaching), I see teachers negotiating the tightrope of writing with their students.

When teachers offer a degree of freedom to students to write about matters close to their hearts, they open a gate to the exploration of emotions and revelations of personal lives in ways that even experienced teachers can find unpredictable and overwhelming. Creating the safe environment necessary for students to explore genuine concerns in their writing requires the teacher to have strong coping skills. At a time when beginning teachers must establish themselves in their classrooms, their personas as writers within the classroom writing community can be a help or hindrance.

Carolann writes with her classes as a way of situating herself in the midst of their struggles as writers:

> If I'm telling them that they have to write poems, then I am going to share a poem with them that I've written. . . . I think it makes a big difference. Because then I'm part of it, too. I'm not just the instructor up here telling them what to do, I'm participating.

She uses her writing to help her students get over a fear of making errors. By showing them her own early drafts and revisions, she clearly establishes the expectation that good writers do not necessarily get it "right" the first time.

This sort of demonstration of process and values seems such common sense that we sometimes overlook the inherent power relations and subtle cues that can bedevil teacher-student relations. Jay, while in his second year of teaching, was aware of such matters and drew a careful line in sharing his own writing with students. He used his essays of literary criticism, written as a university student, as models for his classes, but did not openly share his writing in fiction and poetic forms. He did, however, occasionally cross this line anonymously, by putting his own poetry on the board as quotations for optional prompts for weekly journal writing. One group of Grade 11 girls, with whom he had had constant difficulty throughout the term, admired the poetry:

> And they were actually writing down one of the poems I had up there. But I didn't tell them. . . . I just thought, if I put my name up there it would destroy everything because they wouldn't be able to separate it from me. They wouldn't be able to be objective about it.

While it may be argued that the revelation of his authorship could have helped his relationship with these girls, ultimately only Jay could make this judgment call. In the context of his teaching, this anonymous authorship may well have been essential to his authority.

In process orientations to teaching English language arts, Courtland (1990) points out that the teacher herself is a resource. To rely upon oneself as the teaching resource is a huge risk, particularly for beginning teachers, who may be unsure of themselves as teachers and possibly as writers. The teacher assumes a dual status as teacher and text. When teachers share their writing with students, their writing texts become artifacts that authenticate the teachers as authors and authorities, in the best sense of the word. At a time when beginning teachers must establish their expertise with students, such writing texts can serve many purposes. Teachers thus make resources for present and future teaching, but it is a risky venture. Teachers who foster and participate in a writing community can be, as Jay felt, highly vulnerable. While a writing teacher can dramatically develop his *author-ity* in writing with students, a large dollop of courage is needed also.

The teacher's authority, both in his or her own eyes and in the eyes of the students, is bound to their mutual perception of the teacher's expertise, and this perception is now further complicated by the introduction of new technologies into our writing worlds and classrooms. The stance of authority with which a teacher is invested—willingly or not—in a writing class shifts somewhat when students work in newer forms of writing, such as online and multimedia forms. While the teacher's authority as arbiter of competence in form and genre in the conventional writing classroom (as distinct from the personal authority that all teachers must establish) is rarely called into question (Welch 1998), this naturally understood and accepted authority is less entrenched as students work with newer media and in new forms. As teachers, we are all attempting to understand and exploit the possibilities and new conventions available to us in these new forms, and it is certainly the case in some classrooms that our students' expertise in writing for new media surpasses our own.

This compromised authority of the teacher, with liberating as well as constraining consequences, results whenever students have real audiences for their compositions. When students write in new media, however, the teacher's authority is doubly compromised, both with the provision of real audiences and with the teacher's lack of expertise in the "traditions" of the newer forms. Additionally, and perhaps more disconcertingly, the audiences at times are also quite "unauthorized," as they are unknown and unknowable to students and teachers. Individual teachers must decide what stances of authority—positively or negatively construed—are available and comfortable for them as they work with students in multimedia and online forms.

THE TIGHTROPE OF RESPONSE AND EVALUATION

The dilemma of evaluation inevitably arises when we offer students choice and some degree of freedom in writing. The threat of evaluation has the power to stunt all growth in writing. I am more and more convinced of the central role of evaluation in driving teaching practices, particularly in the current climate of "accountability" and standardized examinations.

Within my university-based writers' workshops, I require and evaluate a varied portfolio of each student's writing. Inevitably, a comment that surfaces in one form or another is, "This is the first poem I've written since junior high. I'm really proud of it. But how can you mark it when it is my own feeling?" The balancing act of responding to and evaluating writing is one of the most difficult to address in the teaching of writing, and arguably, it is the balance upon which all others hinge in one way or another. The false distinction between "creative writing" and "other writing" (ostensibly "not creative"?) has been carefully nurtured in many of our school classrooms and on provincial tests. Creative writing can take on the aura of the sacred: Students often believe that such writing is so personal and so expressive of one's inner being that it cannot be discussed, held up for close examination, or, certainly, evaluated. It is "subjective," and therefore seems untouchable. However, if we subscribe to this view, we distort not only creative writing but all other writing as well. This view leaves "other writing" to the realm of the "objective," which supposedly can be evaluated without pain or emotional investment.

The mystique of "creative" versus "other" writing renders all writing poorer and deprives teachers of our best means of helping students to develop their language abilities. When writing is too precious to be appraised with rigor and evaluated, paradoxically it becomes not at all important. We learn the lessons we are taught: When creative writing is not evaluated, it is not important to students. For many secondary English language arts teachers, the "objective" writing of literary essays is more comfortable to assign and evaluate. But this polarization of kinds of writing based upon a view of the author's emotional investment in the writing is neither productive for the development of language abilities nor true to excellent writing in any form or genre. By using James Britton's (1970) model of language use to distinguish between the expressive language of a diary, for example, and the poetic language of a work of fiction or poetry, we can help our students (of any age) to look at the differences between purely expressive language and shaped, crafted language. We also make the point that some writing *is* indeed too personal to share or examine, and that such writing is valuable for the writer but perhaps does not contribute to the shared experience of school writing. Most productively, we can help our students to explore the boundaries and connections between various uses of language in their writing.

But how do we strike a balance between supportive response and evaluation of writing? How do we feel confident evaluating something more personal than an essay of pseudoliterary criticism? If we cannot tread carefully on this tightrope, we run the risk of forcing students into dead formulaic writing to make our evaluative roles easier: If I don't give you a chance to write about something you care about, I won't risk hurting you. I will, however, teach you that writing is a meaningless activity designed to demonstrate mastery of punctuation rather than to communicate with humanity. James Britton dubbed such writing "dummy runs."

Sometimes, with the best of motives, we distort the complexities of writing. Two high school–level teachers, working in quite different school contexts, discuss their writing instruction in strikingly similar ways. These two teachers—one teaching in a highly academic high school and the other teaching adult upgrading courses—both look for ways to allay their students' fears about writing the external standardized examinations that Alberta students must pass to graduate. Both try to make writing a series of "easy steps" that can be chunked down with writing exercises. However, in presentations of such chunkable steps, both teachers risk presenting a truncated view of writing to their students. A line popularly attributed to Albert Einstein is relevant here: "Everything should be made as simple as possible, but not simpler." Writing is a complex enterprise, and though we want to give our students some strategies for coping with provincial examinations, we must not present an image of writing that is nothing more than five-paragraph essays and canned exercises.

BALANCING THE ROLES OF AUDIENCES

Process orientations to writing suggest that teachers must seek and provide wider audiences for student writing. As Cara realized from seeing her letter in print, such real audiences—from peers to parents to community and beyond—do foster a commitment to the piece of writing. While teachers may struggle to reduce, justify, or sidestep their perceived authority as evaluators, there is little doubt in their minds or in those of their students that the authority is there. The introduction of wider audiences—both known and unknown—for our students' work has an impact on response and evaluation too. Such audiences also contextualize a teacher's response as merely one among many possible responses.

The social dimension of writers' workshop classrooms has often been sentimentalized in an idyllic, romantic vision of individuals engaged in heartfelt writing, supported by congenial and sensitive peers. However, as Lensmire (1994a, 1994b), Dyson (1997), Finders (1997), and others have pointed out, this vision does not adequately represent the social complexity of classrooms of students at any age. Our students exist within a complex web of social and cultural relations, and no teacher can assure all students of the right audiences for their writing. How does a student with less confidence than Angela struggle to retain ownership of his work at the hands of well-meaning but overly zealous peers? What happens to the child who has no friends in a class, and therefore has difficulty seeking such congenial and productive peer conferences with classmates? What happens to the student whose writing defeats even well-intentioned young peer conference partners by its poverty of imagination, overwhelming errors, and so forth? And what about malice?

The introduction of unknown audiences through the use of online and multimedia writing adds additional elements of benefit and risk for young writers. Students can access audiences keenly immersed in and knowledgeable about their own interests, no matter how geographically isolated the writers or how arcane the interests. Some adolescents, and adults alike, feel "most freely and honestly" themselves only in online conversations, where such essentializing qualities as race, age, gender, and physical appearance can be ignored (Tobin, 1998, p. 122). For adolescent and teenage writers who feel marginalized in their social milieux, as well as those with unusual areas of interest and expertise, the opportunity to focus on the communication and to ignore essentializing aspects can be powerfully attractive. Eliza Dresang (1997) notes:

> The online forums extend the sense of authenticity and connection that is so motivating to young people—what they have to say will be heard and in some cases responded to by other young people across the world. Online experiences encourage spontaneity and provide both opportunities for youth to test their own voices and outlets for their creativity and their curiosity in a public place. (p. 11)

But online writing also provides opportunities for the creation of fictitious identities in cyberspace locations, as Michael Lewis (2001) vividly illustrates in his portrait of a popular Internet "legal expert," who happened to be a teenager with no legal credentials. If we assist students in accessing wider audiences, we also must seek a balance to make our students "cyberwise" enough to have strategies to assess credibility and protect themselves from sinister cyberspace correspondents, while also avoiding misrepresenting themselves in ways that could have serious repercussions.

THE COUNTERBALANCE IN INDIVIDUAL AND COLLABORATIVE WRITING

The balances that we may seek to achieve in the conventional process-writing classroom, however, are more fundamentally being shaken by technological developments. Chris Anson (1999) states, "In the context of our beliefs about how students best learn to write, many educators are haunted . . . by a sense that bigger things are happening around us as we continue to refine classroom methods and tinker with our teaching styles" (p. 262). Anson comments upon the stability, notwithstanding the advent of computers, of "the textual landscape of writing instruction" (p. 262). While computers have made serious revision of drafts of writing so much easier to accomplish and have made information easier to access, teachers have not, for the most part, reconceptualized the texts or processes we have taught students.

One balance that shifts dramatically when students work online and in hypermedia is that of individual and collaborative writing. Our traditional vision of a solitary writer, or an individual contributor to a group project, often leads us merely to divide up tasks at hand into coordinated and individual pieces of larger projects rather than to teach students to synthesize integral contributions to a collaborative effort. Yet online and hypermedia forms themselves invite collaboration, as does the contemporary corporate world. New Canadian programs of study in English language arts place a degree of emphasis, in various terminologies, upon information management. Such management needs to develop beyond cut-and-paste jobs. Information gathering has become easier with access to online technology and writing from the Internet, but unfortunately, glib cut-and-paste jobs by one or several students are also easier to accomplish.

Real collaborative writing does not develop spontaneously but requires a range of interpersonal, technical, and writing skills. As we move into this area to teach students writing skills for new technologies and new adult work contexts, we will need to tread this tightrope carefully. With more collaborative writing transpiring across wider geographical spaces, we will need to be alert to developing the necessary interpersonal skills to accomplish such writing in productive ways.

WALKING THE TIGHTROPE

When Joyce wrote of feeling like a tightrope walker, she had in mind the insecurities of beginning to teach. But teachers of writing, no matter how experienced, navigate the tightrope continually. Working in both capacities as teacher and as writer—as a writing teacher and a teacher writing—we can achieve balance, though perhaps only momentarily. When we are only the teacher or only the writer, we overbalance of necessity. When we do both, we can establish a delicate balance. Like tightrope walkers, we continually adjust to the pull of opposing forces to achieve our moments of equilibrium.

NOTE

I acknowledge with gratitude the support of both the Social Sciences and Humanities Research Council of Canada and the Faculty of Education Alumni Fund—Literacy for the Twenty-first Century Initiative for funding the research discussed in this chapter. I wish to thank the teachers for permission to quote their writing and their conversations.

REFERENCES

Anson, C. M. (1999). Distant voices: Teaching and writing in a culture of technology. *College English, 61*(3), 261–280.

Atwell, N. (1987). *In the middle: Writing, reading and learning with adolescents.* Portsmouth, NH: Boynton/Cook.

Britton, J. (1970). *Language and learning.* Harmondsworth, England: Penguin Books.

Britton, J., et al. (1975). *The development of writing abilities (11–18).* London: Macmillan.

Calkins, L. M. (1991). *Living between the lines.* Portsmouth, NH: Heinemann.

Courtland, M. C. (1990). *The process of teacher change in literacy instruction.* Paper presented at the 10th Invitational Conference of the Canadian Association of Curriculum Studies, Lethbridge, AB.

Dresang, E. T. (1997). Developing student voices on the Internet. *Book Links, 7*(1), 10–15.

Dyson, A. H. (1997). *Writing superheroes: Contemporary childhood, popular culture, and classroom literacy.* New York: Teachers College Press.

Finders, M. J. (1997). *Just girls: Hidden literacies and life in junior high.* Urbana, IL: National Council of Teachers of English.

Graves, D. (1985). *Writing: Teachers and children at work.* Portsmouth, NH: Heinemann.

Kirby, D., Liner, T., & Vinz, R. (1988). *Inside out: Developmental strategies for teaching writing.* Portsmouth, NH: Boynton/Cook.

Lensmire, T. J. (1994a). *When children write: Critical re-visions of the writing workshop.* New York: Teachers College Press.

Lensmire, T. J. (1994b). Writing workshop as carnival: Reflections on an alternative learning environment. *Harvard Educational Review, 64*(4), 371–391.

Lewis, M. (2001, July 15). Faking it. *New York Times Magazine,* pp. 32–37, 44, 61–63.

Murray, D. (1985). *A writer teaches writing* (2nd ed.). Boston: Houghton Mifflin.

Romano, T. (1987). *Clearing the way.* Portsmouth, NH: Heinemann.

Tobin, J. (1998). An American *Otaku:* (or, a boy's virtual life on the net). In J. Sefton-Green (Ed.), *Digital diversions: Youth culture in the age of multimedia.* London: UCL Press.

Vinz, R. (1993). *Composing a teaching life: Partial, multiple, and sometimes contradictory representations of teaching and learning literature.* Urbana, IL: National Council of Teachers of English.

Welch, N. (1998). Sideshadowing teacher response. *College English, 60*(4), 374–95.

CHAPTER 7

"Trying to Bend the Tree When It Is Already Grown": Spanning the Spectrum of African Diaspora Englishes in the College Writing Classroom

CARMEN KYNARD
Medgar Evers College, City University of New York

> *The argument concerning the use, or the status, or the reality, of Black English is rooted in American history and has absolutely nothing to do with the question the argument supposes itself to be posing. The argument has nothing to do with language itself but with the role of language. Language, incontestably, reveals the speaker. . . . It is not the Black child's language that is in question, it is not his language that is despised: It is his experience.*
> —James Baldwin, "If Black English Isn't a Language, Then Tell Me, What Is?"

In my first days of teaching writing at the college level, Ngũgĩ wa Thiong'o's book *Decolonising the Mind: The Politics of Language in African Literature* was my source of solace. I spent much of my first 2 years teaching Freshman Composition severely depressed by what I saw being masqueraded as education for the Black and Latino college students before me. Today, I continue to turn to thinkers like Ngũgĩ who have taught me that if the aim of writing is to question the underlying assumptions and structures behind the social systems we have inherited, then our schools' language policies, both implicit and explicit, must also be interrogated.

Ngũgĩ argues that "language as communication, the written" is what served the most "affective area of domination." This domination is not simply about school enforcing a language or dialect different from the home. Writing is employed to reproduce not only a certain language, but the world, ideals, and hierarchies constructed in that language (Ngũgĩ, 1986, p. 17). When it comes to school, language and ideology are always inseparable. This intellectual tradition thus serves as a foundation for my thinking about the history of African diaspora language varieties, language pedagogy, and most important, the social, political, and intellectual purposes of writing, as I attempt to push beyond the usual clamoring for simplistic how-to protocols for helping students read, write, and speak "better."

This chapter centers on students' writing, schooling experiences, and spoken and written styles. I refer to a wide variety of African Diaspora English speakers: Puerto Rican students who locate their African American Vernacular English (AAVE) use alongside their Puerto Rican English; Dominican students who call themselves Afro-Hispanic AAVE speakers and so see themselves as beyond being just bilingual ("in case ya don't know, now ya do" as one student proclaimed); Anglophone Caribbean students who dispute the terms *broken English* and *patois;* and U.S. African Americans who proclaim that Hip-Hop is their primary vernacular. The term *African Diaspora Englishes* is borrowed from scholars like Paul Gilroy and Robin Kelley who argue that the identities of African diaspora people are transnational, fluid, hybrid, dynamic, and overlapping, which keeps them in constant dialogue with each other and the social world. This perspective encourages teaching that allows such speakers to be "active agents" rather than passive victims in grossly simplistic interpretations of a type of singular monolithic Black culture and language system (Kelley, 1997).

In the first section of this chapter, I highlight the experience of a struggling writer. In the second, I explore the contradictions that have emerged out of discussions of African Diaspora Englishes in the classroom. In the final section, I consider how sophisticated writers use many English registers across a wide range of their writings. This progression along different points of the spectrum allows me to round out how African Diaspora Englishes affect the full range of our classroom encounters, while critiquing where I myself need to venture.

PREVENTING STUDENTS FROM WRITING THE ACADEMY

The Antilles Negro who wants to be white will be the whiter as he gains greater mastery of the cultural tool that language is.
—Frantz Fanon, *Black Skins, White Masks*

When I began teaching college writing at the City University of New York, I imagined a classroom where my students would use writing to explore social and political issues of relevance to the lived realities of the global Black masses. They would thereby forge a space and meaning for themselves at the university to affirm their voices and unique experiences in the Western world. While I was immersed in a questioning process of the sociopolitical deconstruction of modes of discourse (narrative, persuasive, compare and contrast, and so forth) and the "analytic, nonpersonal academic voice" in college writing, I never imagined plunging so directly into thinking about language. Student stories and insights revealed schooling and language not to be accidental repetitions across the African diaspora, but instead rooted in historical colonialism. In that sense my attempt to understand these accounts grounds my critique of the hyperparanoid fascination with surface error that inflicts many of the spaces inside the institution where I work. The danger of instructors' error-hunting practices, particularly when coupled with the racism that views non-Anglo students as linguistically and cognitively deficient, lies in the fact that this is what produces errors and nonwriters in the first place. The story of a struggling writer thus serves to anchor one end of the spectrum that I will be exploring.

Like many of my students, Sherrie did not see herself as someone who wrote well. She cited her grammar, handwriting, and spelling as reasons for this, with the self-proclaimed issue of subject-verb agreement her biggest foe in the enterprise of school writing. At the beginning of the semester, in her informal journals she would write two verb forms for the subjects of each of her sentences and circle one of them, which was usually "wrong." I had never seen anything like it. Every noun had two verbs in parentheses—her writing looked like a handout from a grammar workbook. When I asked Sherrie about this circling, she said that when she writes, she can't decide which verb form to choose so she puts both in brackets and goes back afterwards to circle one. I suggested she write what comes to mind first and then we'd go back and examine her patterns. She must not have liked this idea because she continued to write two verb forms as before, only now she left them uncircled, writing me notes at the bottom asking *me* to circle the right answer. Sherrie produced very little writing, using short, choppy sentences that lacked clarity, voice, and complexity. She stopped the practice of doubling every verb by the end of the semester, but she still insisted that she would never understand subject-verb agreement and that she was a horrible, messy writer. When I showed her one of my own messy drafts, she simply laughed and told me I was crazy.

Our conversations throughout the semester suggested that deep "lessons" had been internalized by Sherrie based on the writing and language pedagogy in her life. Sherrie's burden of self-inflicted grammar exercises was very reminiscent of Sondra Perl's study (1979/1994) that described basic writers so focused on error correction that they were unable to move forward in their writing. At the beginning of the semester, Sherrie was one of the more outspoken advocates of speaking "proper English," or what she called "ethical English." By the second month, however, Sherrie began telling different autobiographical accounts of her language history. I provided a variety of articles about language and students were directed to choose one and discuss the issues it raised in a small group. I deliberately included writers who employ what Louise Rodríguez Connal (2000) calls *transcultural rhetorics:* "writing that crosses and includes multiple languages, genres, and styles for people who affiliate with two or more cultures, languages, or dialects" (p. 321).

Sherrie chose the introduction to one of Geneva Smitherman's (2000) books, a chapter entitled "From Ghetto Lady to Critical Linguist," noting how silence is internalized when speech is constantly corrected:

> Geneva Smitherman states that she made it through school by keeping her mouth shut. This statement made me think of myself because that was the way I was growing up. . . . only when I was around my friends did I speak. I guess because I felt like they understood me and they never corrected me because they spoke the same way.

The final issue that came up was sheer confusion as to how Smitherman could be such a good writer *and* scholar and still pride herself as an AAVE speaker. This made no sense for Sherrie. "What's the deal with that?" she questioned repeatedly in her journal. In response to the formal essay assignment—analyze one or two of the texts read and discussed in the course so far—Sherrie chose Smitherman and produced the most fluent writing I had seen her do.

After this paper Sherrie no longer argued for the recognition of "proper" or "ethical" English. In fact, in one of our last, private conversations, we were talking about a media presentation on child abuse when out of the blue Sherrie exclaimed how English class often feels like child abuse: You walk on eggshells, timid and nervous, because any little mistake will set things off and get you punished. In this dialogue with Sherrie I decided to really listen to her speech patterns. I expected to hear the forms she is so hypersensitive to in her writing, yet her speech never once reflected the subject-verb grammatical patterns of AAVE ("she don't" for "he doesn't" or copula absence). Walking to the classroom together, she immediately began chatting with her friends in the hall. I eavesdropped on these conversations, wondering if Sherrie saw me as a knuckles-slapping English teacher and therefore self-edited her expression. Again, no AAVE patterns in her speech. I listened closely to her verbal responses in class with the same result. So why does Sherrie get so confused about surface issues not reflected in her speech? How has this become the site of her "dialect interference"—a phenomena she can even name, suggesting that it was something taught to her, for who walks around talking about dialect interference except English language arts teachers? Do we have a case of pedagogical abuse, where the very diagnosis has led to the symptoms? This is reminiscent of Jerrie Cobb Scott's (1993) argument that speakers of nonmainstream dialects are hypersensitive to their need to "monitor their written expressions" (p. 337). This is not the innate tendency of a dialect speaker, but a practice learned from school, specifically from the English classroom.

Perhaps at some point in Sherrie's school life, she actually experienced problems with subject-verb agreement. Yet as a student in college, where were these continual diagnoses of dialect interference coming from? This is not to say that Sherrie's writing does not reflect AAVE patterns. However, these patterns are aspects of her rhetorical, argumentative style that, as Arnetha Ball (1992) has shown, involves special circumlocution, narrative interspersion, and recursion, which reflect models of African American sermons or other expressive oral genres.

Sherrie, make no mistake about it, is a speaker of African American English. Her phonology and modes of discourse have marked her among her teachers. As Bailey and Thomas (1998) argue, the phonological features of AAVE play a critical role in the assignment of a disproportionate percentage of African Americans to special education classes. Phonology itself often serves to ethnically identify African Americans, with intonation alone demarcating Black speech patterns. In short, phonology clears a path for discriminatory practices against African American language speakers (p. 86). Sherrie's speech, for example, shows these features:

- Final consonant cluster reduction (hand > han; first > firs; boyfriend > boyfren)
- Vocalization of postvocalic /l/ (well > we)
- Labialization of interdental fricatives; substitution of /f,v/ (mother > muvver; with > wit; mouth > mouf)

More importantly, Sherrie's language also exhibits what Geneva Smitherman (1977) describes as *tonal semantics:* talk-singing, repetitive and alliterative word-play, intonational contouring, and rhyme. When students such as Sherrie start "breakin' it down" in the classroom, it is perceived as antithetical to sophisticated, academic analysis.

While Sherrie struggled throughout the semester, it was "decolonising" her ideas about language through the use of Smitherman's text that allowed her to finally write. Centering African Diaspora Englishes in this case is about students exploring how racism at the site of their Englishes positions them outside of writing. Working with such students ultimately demands my own activism at the institutional level, where repression begins, not just meeting with Sherrie one-on-one. Each semester in my department, faculty attempt to fail students' exam essays based on what they refer to as "annoying personal digressions," some of which are clear examples of "the three patterns that emerge in the expository language of African-American students: circumlocution, narrative interspersion, and recursion" (Ball, 1992, p. 509). These are always questioned by the instructors and serve as a reason for students repeating freshman writing even though the exam question itself asks for personal connections. This recycles Ford's research from 1984, where white teachers rated compositions with Spanish features lower than compositions with Standard American English features even when those essays contained more complex ideas than the essays written in Standard English. Similarly, in a 1973 study Williams showed that white teachers in Chicago and Memphis consistently stereotyped AAVE speakers as unsuccessful in school based on their utterances on a tape, while white teachers in Texas did the same for Chicano English speakers (both studies discussed in McGroarty, 1996, p. 16). In a parallel study, Ana C. Zentella (1997) shows that nonstandard forms in a piece of writing gain such conspicuousness that they appear more widespread than they actually are (p. 173). Given a similar picture on the campuses where I meet students like Sherrie, I obviously need to find a way to intervene in their schooling beyond just noticing the ways they defeat themselves as writers.

STUDENTS LOCATING AND THEORIZING THE MOTHER TONGUE

Of course we must learn English but I think that Jamaican people have more to say in their language than in English. It is the language of the country. It is three hundred years we been talking it. It is not a corruption of anything. It is, mind you, a regional dialect because it belongs to an island, we can't expect everybody to understand it. After all, English only start 'pon a little island over there and we still learn it.
—Louise Bennett in an interview with Nesha Haniff (1991)

I often start a semester by asking students to write about a personal memory involving a school experience that stands out strongly for them. We then read these stories in class to uncover the political and sociohistorical circumstances for what students have encountered. Ultimately stories about race, class, and language discrimination emerge. This is not to say that schooling's institutionalized language discrimination only occurs at the college level: the principal of my former high school, an African American woman who only wore Saks Fifth Avenue business suits with shoes to match, would pull students out of my classroom and ask them to stop using so much AAVE. At the urban, public university where I teach, everyday I walk into a room full of students who are bombarded by speech classes, entry writing exams, proficiency exams, incessant grammar and usage drills, monologues about the importance of good grammar over content, and departmental midterms and final exams. These fortifications blockade students from the academy because their written or spoken speech can be labeled *nonstandard*, or shown to exhibit "incorrect" usage and grammar, "ESL issues," or "dialect interference."

Students who represent Anglophone Caribbean and Africa relate horror stories much in line with the kind of schooling Ngũgĩ describes in colonial Kenya. There continue to be students who report being told routinely by their college instructors—individually as well as collectively in a lecture format—that they will not do well because of their "language problems"; students who say they feel that they are not called on in class because they have an "accent"; students whose grades have been explicitly lowered in speech classes because of their "accents"; students who are publicly reprimanded for their use of "dialect" in the classroom. Curiously, dreadlock-adorned and African art–decorating professors are also enforcers. Then there are the everyday discursive practices where the casual discussions among instructors center on students' inability to speak or write. A group of white male professors once told me that this was the fault of rap music since this was really just "second-grade baby talk." Unfortunately, these responses are not racist aberrations of a few professors, but consistent occurrences. As Keith Gilyard (1991) contends in *Voices of the Self*, which theorizes, historicizes, and politicizes his own literacy autobiography, the college classroom reproduces the purposes of the elite instead of ameliorating social inequality, and language is one of the key mechanisms for accomplishing this.

Unlike many of my U.S. African American students, students from the Caribbean have a meta-awareness of the various dialect registers they use, including knowing they have an "accent," no matter what part of the Creole Continuum (Rickford, 1987) they are straddling. The basic premise of the Creole Continuum is that there are no sharp cleavages between Creole and Standard English; rather a continuous array of speech varieties range from the basilect (the most conservative Creole) to the mesolect (midranges and less creolized) to the acrolect (the standard variety with some local phonological and lexical features).

Ironically many U.S. African American students routinely devalue AAVE in the very same utterances in which they use it, an occurrence much rarer for students from the Anglophone Caribbean and Africa. I do not mean to overromanticize the politicizing of language for Anglophone Caribbean and African students because many are equally wedded to their Creoles being largely broken English instead of containing rule-governed, systematic linguistic structures. However, the linguistic consciousness of such students who span the African diaspora has stimulated in my classroom lively debates about language. U.S. African American students often become more aware of language use by listening to their peers from the Caribbean, while Anglophone Caribbean and African students, who see their own languages as more divergent from the standard than AAVE, begin to question the politics of race and schooling in their new U.S. homes.

In a journal entry that asked students to free associate with the concept of Mother Tongue, Uzo, a Nigerian woman and Pidgin speaker, wrote:

> Mother Tongue is more like a culture, or a means of identity for the people who use it. Most times it is a means for one to feel s/he belongs to a group. There are many of them and each one has its own set of meanings. . . . When I speak my Mother's Tongue the beauty of it is what I bring across to others, my expressions, gestures, and tone when I'm speaking all mean something and the person I speak it to understands every expression I make and responds.

These ideas were very different from those of an African American student that semester who refused to even acknowledge AAVE. James ardently believed AAVE was not something to be discussed, that there were simply such things as correct and incorrect. By the end of the semester, however, James told the class he had completely changed his mind and was extremely angry for having been taught that his language was incorrect and improper. After listening to these non-U.S. students describe language, James could see AAVE speakers as inventing language, not disregarding its rules and, thereby, its sanctity. It was nothing that I did or said that challenged him; rather, it was his participation in a group that focused on the life and work of Louise Bennett, more affectionately called Miss Lou, the national poetess of Jamaica who was the first to write and perform poetry for a national audience in Jamaican "nation language," not "dialect," "broken English," or "patois"—derogatory terms Brathwaite (1984) argues against. James could now see and understand the ways in which issues of deviancy and correct-incorrect are always already a social construction and, within the reality of the United States, it will be intimately connected to race. Thus he moved beyond his self-reflexive hatred of AAVE.

Uzo, the author of the previous journal entry on "Mother Tongue," raises other issues. What does it mean when she values Mother Tongue but not in the writing she submits to her college teachers? For Uzo, as long as she got good grades, things were okay. Students like her—and those like her who are not so grade-fortunate—have described the intricate workings of how they dissect the instructor's desires and spit it back to them. This is how they connect to writing. Whenever I use Nesha Haniff's interview with Louise Bennett, the line "Of course we must learn English but I think that Jamaican people have more to say in their language than in English" is quickly embraced by students, especially when I do a text-rendering session. Again, what has happened when students see themselves as having something to say in Jamaican or patois but not in the language of their writing?

These discussions and written narratives of my students in response to language and their schooling suggest that they experience language in U.S. college classrooms in ways similar to Ngũgĩ's descriptions of colonialism in Kenya. Centering African Diaspora Englishes in this instance is about questioning supersimplistic notions of writing and discourse where brain-numbing boundaries and binaries get constructed: formal and informal, home and school, academic and vernacular. It's as if writing is the same thing as making 10-minute store-bought spaghetti—just drain off the excess water from the pasta and add sauce at the end. Language and discourses don't get cooked up in separate pots and then run through aluminum strainers where you shake away the dialect from the standard in textual productions. Constructing words and meanings are not that simple. Yet we often talk about it this way. All of which produces the kind of simplistic and alienating writing identities that characterize the students described here.

Instead of simply being the place for *developing* writing and language skills, can the composition classroom be the place for *exploring* language use and power? As Gilyard (1996) has argued, reading and writing act "powerfully upon us; at the same time, we can act powerfully on and through reading, writing, and instruction" (p. 24). Are the rules of writing really bottom-up, where one must first learn every standard convention before being able to explore and deviate? Who controls exploration and deviation in this model? Is this really the most generative model we can imagine for the human mind's capacity—a capitalistic hierarchy where one begins with a small chunk of capital, invests it, and then watches as it grows and grows until finally one can deviate and possess Trump Towers? The question for me is not how to help students arrive at the version of English academics have determined, but how students can configure themselves in English and move on to the other end of the spectrum.

THE TREE IS ALREADY GROWN

Language is political. That's why you and me, my Brother and Sister, that's why we sposed to choke our natural self into the weird, lying, barbarous, unreal, white speech and writing habits that the schools lay down like holy law. Because in other words, the powerful don't play: they mean to keep that power, and those who are the powerless (you and me) better shape up and mimic/ape/suck-in the very image of the powerful, or the powerful will destroy you—you and your children.
—June Jordan, *On Call: Political Essays* (1985)

I will never forget the response of one student to an excerpt of *Decolonising the Mind*. Sonja expressed her outrage at colonial education policies—forcing anyone to wear a sign reading "I am a donkey" if caught speaking his or her mother tongue—with the following metaphor: "This is an illustration of trying to bend the tree when it is already grown."

A bidialectal approach, which I believe is the dominant method and ideology for dealing with language varieties in the classroom, is still too close to "bending the tree." It suggests you can use your own language at home and on the street (maybe even sometimes for a creative writing assignment). However, at school and in the workplace, you must simply accept the status quo. Since 1969, linguists such as James Sledd (1996) have questioned the politics of White mainstream educators and their middle-class Black counterparts in upholding this type of bidialectalism as a prerequisite for economic opportunity (p. 35). Two equally dangerous lies get promoted to Black children when we make promises of material success via standardized languages. First, we leave too much room for its corollary: namely, that the Black masses in the shantytowns of South Africa, the favelas of Brazil, and the "government yards" of the U.S. and Caribbean (as Bob Marley has labeled the slums of Trenchtown and Wyclef Jean has labeled the slums of New Jersey) are catching hell because they don't know how to code-switch and style-switch. Only a political fool could think this. Second, we suggest to students of the African diaspora that they can reach a larger audience when they change the way they speak and write, without offering the history of writers who have consciously rejected this position or radical thinkers who have remained marginalized even when they have adopted standardized languages. Furthermore, given the history of Emmitt Till, the Little Rock Nine, the Four Little Girls, and Latasha Harlins, I find it a very dangerous thing to tell youth that all dey gotta do is change dem dialects and they will suddenly be heard, understood, and embraced by White institutions.

Inherent in the ideology of bidialectalism is the dangerous notion of language as mere mimicry of the elite. There is no monolithic, stagnant, unchanging, standardized academic discourse where nonmainstream or non-Western writers sift out all traces of their mother tongues. To believe otherwise means one has not read a wide range of academic articles and journals by non-White scholars. Even highly academic writers, all very skilled in Western academic conventions—Ngũgĩ wa Thiong'o, Richard Scott Lyons, Gayatri Spivak, Cornel West—do not construct morphology, lexicon, or syntax in stock, mirror images to "traditional" Western writers or to each other. When we look beyond the most superficial aspects of surface sentence construction, we see that writers do not all argue the same. They do not speak with the same rhythms, intonations, and cadences, and so their words on the page *do* sound differently. They are not discursive clones although this certainly seems to be an aspect of many writing curricula, which often train students for an assembly-line production of one stock essay churned out of the academic writing machine.

Every semester I have a published writer in my classroom: a student on his way to or from the record studio cutting a spoken word or rap album; a poet performing her work at popular cultural venues; a student writing for a local access television or radio station; a student who guides her family in writing children's stories for her children and grandchildren to explore the storytelling traditions of her native Trinidad. Their comments about writing, their connections to writing, and their ability to reinvent themselves and their topics across a variety of domains are always different from most of the students I teach.

These students remind me of the way Gilyard (1996) describes himself as a college writer in his chapter entitled "Playing with the Patterns":

> I had a whole lot to say and didn't have too much trouble saying it. Whatever the assignment was, I bent it to my purposes. That's how I figured you did it. Show teachers enough of their own style, then bend the rest yo' way. Know what I'm sayin? Even if they give you some passé protocols to work with, you cover them, sign them the way Aretha Franklin or Luther Vandross push against commonplace delivery to place their inimitable vocal signatures on ballads. (p. 126)

Like Gilyard, my students at this point on the continuum know they have something peculiar to say, know how to "sign" their own "ballads," have a sense of their own purposes and so *can* bend assignments their own way. They also have some overriding question that guides their social thinking and actions. What is striking here is how these writers have largely been shaped *outside* of the classroom, especially outside of the writing classroom. One cannot help but be struck by all of the poets and activists whom Gilyard knew, organized with, and discoursed with as a college student. Outside of his college school-ing, he has his own world as a member in a variety of communities in which he thinks, writes, and acts to shape his notions of the overriding, sociopolitical questions on which he focuses. These are the types of students who have been my strongest, most experimental, and most engaged writers. They are, of course, not the majority, but they do exist in every classroom in which I have taught.

These writers also remind me of the type of connection to writing that someone like Toni Morrison possesses, who also moves past simplistic, narrow, either-or dichotomies of standard English or dialect:

> So what I do, I have to write in a way that will embrace all the levels of English I grew up with. When any of us were misbehaving badly, my mother would say, "Go somewhere and sit down." Or she might say, "I'm going to knock you into the middle of next week." Or she might say, "Honor thy mother and thy father, that thy days may be long upon the land." Or she might say, "More poisonous than a ser-pent's tooth is an ungrateful child." And I thought all of this language was the same, and it was all mine. So I never felt estranged by standard English, and I never felt uncomfortable with so-called colloquial or vernacular language. All of it was home for me, and that is what I want to render. (quoted in Botstein, 2001, p. 154)

Morrison's sentiment here is very unlike that of Sherrie, who thinks that any-thing that is "so-called colloquial or vernacular language" is literally "unethi-cal." This sentiment is also very much different from those expressed by stu-dents like Uzo, the ones whom I call the "what-the-teacher-wants" PIs (private investigators). These students interpret their college classrooms (albeit, per-haps rightly so) as antithetical to the incorporation of "Mother Tongue" and therefore see the act of writing as antithetical to it also.

Another crucial point for me is that these students have an audience out-side the classroom and a separate system for evaluation that they themselves shape. This allows them to shape a different conception of their writing inside the classroom. They write for themselves and the worlds they see themselves as being able to re-create, not simply the mysterious, simplistic dictates of the teacher in charge. And like Gilyard, depending on what they will be able to get away with in certain classrooms, they push their writing in multiple, hybrid forms in ways that many of their professors (and educational theorists) could only wish to approximate. Many teachers concede that you can write in hybrid forms sometimes (in the right places that they themselves dictate of course) but have no experience or expertise with actually doing it themselves. They talk forever and a day about how much they love Toni Morrison but cannot incor-porate her thinking or style into their own politics of writing. The incessant criers of "learn the code of power" have as many codes to learn as anybody else, given their own monolingualism-monodialectalism and the one-dimensional style of their own writings. These folks advocate restrictions on stuff they can't even do—like teachers talking about how to write fiction but ain't never wrote no fiction themselves.

I acknowledge, however, that I must do much more to create the kind of hybrid, socially complex space in my own classroom, one that would match what sophisticated writers enjoy outside of their classrooms. As I seek to validate this end of the spectrum, I need to keep in mind how the wide range of writing attitudes and performances by my current students only reflects what is often negative writing and writing pedagogy in the present climate. But these same students continue to help me realize what writing and writing pedagogy can be.

REFERENCES

Bailey, G., & Thomas, E. (1998). Some aspects of African American vernacular English phonology. In S. Mufwene, J. Rickford, G. Bailey, & J. Baugh (Eds.), *African American English: Structure, history, and use* (pp. 85–109). New York: Routledge.

Baldwin, J. (1998). If Black English isn't a language, then tell me, what is? In L. Delpit & T. Perry (Eds.), *The real Ebonics debate: Power, language, and the education of African-American children* (pp. 67–70). Boston: Beacon Press. (Original essay published 1979)

Ball, A. (1992). Cultural preference and the expository writing of African American adolescents. *Written Communication, 9*(4), 501–532.

Botstein, L. (2001). Things fall together: A conversation with Chinua Achebe and Toni Morison. *Transition,* no. 89, 150–165.

Brathwaite, K. (1984). *History of the voice.* London: New Beacon Books.

Connal, L. R. (2000). Transcultural rhetorics for survival. In R. D. Gonzales & I. Melis (Eds.), *Language ideologies* (Vol. 1, pp. 318–332). Urbana, IL: National Council of Teachers of English.

Fanon, F. (1991). *Black skins, white masks.* New York: Grove Press. (Original published 1952)

Gilroy, P. (1993). *The Black Atlantic: Double consciousness and modernity.* Cambridge, MA: Harvard University Press.

Gilyard, K. (1991). *Voices of the self: A study of language competence.* Detroit, MI: Wayne State University.

Gilyard, K. (1996). *Let's flip the script: An African American discourse on language, literature, and learning.* Detroit, MI: Wayne State University.

Haniff, N. (1991). Miss Lou. In C. Sunshine (Ed.), *Caribbean connections: Jamaica* (pp. 61–62). Washington, DC: Network of Educators' Committees on Central America.

Jordan, J. (1985). *On call: Political essays.* Boston: South End Press.

Kelley, R. (1997). *Yo' mama's disfunktional: Fighting the culture wars in urban America.* Boston: Beacon Press.

McGroarty, M. (1996). Language attitudes, motivations, and standards. In S. McKay & N. Hornberger (Eds.), *Sociolinguistics and language teaching* (pp. 3–46). Cambridge, UK: Cambridge University Press.

Ngũgĩ wa Thiong'o. (1986). *Decolonising the mind: The politics of language in African literature.* Portsmouth, NH: Heinemann.

Perl, S. (1994). The composing processes of unskilled college writers. In S. Perl (Ed.), *Landmark essays on writing process.* Davis, CA: Hermagoras Press. (Original essay published 1979)

Rickford, J. R. (1987). *Dimensions of a creole continuum.* Stanford, CA: Stanford University Press.

Scott, J. C. (1993). Accommodating nonmainstream language in the composition classroom. In A. W. Glowka & D. M. Lance (Eds.), *Language variation in North American English: Research and teaching* (pp. 331–345). New York: Modern Language Association.

Sledd, J. (1996). *Eloquent dissent: The writings of James Sledd* (R. Freed, Ed.). Portsmouth, NH: Heinemann.

Smitherman, G. (1977). *Talkin' and testifyin': The language of Black America.* Boston: Houghton Mifflin.

Smitherman, G. (2000). *Talkin' that talk: Language, culture, and education in African America.* New York: Routledge.

Zentella, A. (1997). *Growing up bilingual: Puerto Rican children in New York.* Malden, MA: Blackwell.

CHAPTER 8

Developing Critical Responses to Stories in Many Media

MARGARET MACKEY
University of Alberta

Scene: I am in a school workroom with four other people. Two of them are Grade-9 students, a boy and a girl. The other two are my graduate research assistants. We are videotaping the two students as they play *Starship Titanic,* Douglas Adams's complex narrative computer game. Jack is an experienced game player; Alexis has never taken an interest in computer games. My graduate assistants mirror this gender gap to some degree. Dave, the camera operator, has played many games, though not as many as Jack. Joanne, the note taker, is very familiar with CD-ROM encyclopedias and is a master of the Internet, but she is not much of a game player. I am probably somewhere in the middle of this spectrum, but my game-playing instincts are hard-won through observation of many different players and through assistance from my children; I have never put in the hours of playing that it would take to make the processes intuitive.

Jack is a whiz. He saves his game compulsively, every 90 seconds or so, and when he runs into a problem he simply abandons the game and retreats to the last point saved. He does this so automatically that the process is clearly transparent to him and does not interfere with his sense of narrative progress in the slightest. He speeds through the narrative intricacies of the plot with a keen eye for salient details.

Alexis has never thought of such a tactic as constantly saving the game and admires its simplicity and efficacy. Dave, Joanne, and I are similarly impressed with Jack's speed and skill. I am reminded of two other Grade-9 students who played this game for us the previous week. I asked them if they thought of this computer game as a story. "It might be like a story if we didn't make so many mistakes," they said. Jack has established a way of smoothing over the mistakes, backing out of blind alleys so swiftly that the effect is one of almost effortless forward progression—almost like reading.

I describe this scene in such detail because it led me to think very seriously about how classrooms can work when the balance of expertise is tipped in favor of some but not all of the students. Of the five people in the room, Jack was by far the most experienced, the most resourceful, and the most successful in processing this particular narrative. My two graduate assistants talked all the way back to the university about how they could hardly wait to take another crack at *Starship Titanic*, utilizing the strategies they had observed in Jack and in other student players. With our widely varying range of understanding and expertise, all four of the rest of us in that room had registered that we had learned something useful about text processing.

Some version of this scene takes place in many classrooms where work is being done with computers. If the teacher is not in a position to devote many out-of-school hours to computer work and play, he or she will almost certainly be teaching students who are more experienced, whose intuitions have been at-tuned to the specific criteria that make a computer program work successfully. The plain reality of English teaching is that it eats teachers' time. Even those who are knowledgeable about computers are unlikely to be able to invest the same number of hours in exploring new alternatives as their students will do on a nightly basis.

Similarly, in many other areas that draw on different forms of popular cul-ture, students will simply know more than their teachers. There is an astonish-ing amount of information about popular culture readily available to those with the time to spend. In a study I conducted of different texts associated with one single movie, *Men in Black*, I came up with a set of more than 60 print sources, mostly specialist magazines. Some of these journals elucidated particular tech-nological challenges of making such a movie, describing the making of the com-puter graphics, the development of the special effects makeup, and the creation of the sound track. Others provided background information on the actors, the director, the producer, the original comic book artist whose story was adapted for the film, and so forth. A third set explored the science-fiction elements of the story and explained the urban mythology of the men in black. This plethora of print sources does not represent the end of the story. Anyone with an interest in this particular film could have watched many television programs, such as *Entertainment Tonight*, featuring interviews with the actors and the other people associated with the making of this movie, and providing backstage visits to the production stage and workshops. Furthermore, a vast range of similar and sup-plementary information was readily available on the Internet. Expertise in the subject of the making of *Men in Black* would really only call for the marshalling of a requisite degree of interest and, of course, for the investment of time.

Students know that they are better informed about many topics than many of their teachers. They may presume (and all too often presume rightly) that their teachers will answer this expertise with a devaluing of the kinds of topics about which kids know more than adults. How many English curricula give credit for advanced skills in the processing of the texts of computer games? What value is ascribed to the accumulation of trivia about Hollywood ways of moviemaking as opposed to (say) information about the floor plan of the Globe Theatre in sixteenth-century London?

I am not arguing for a minute that English teachers should cede all ground to the interests of their students and teach only texts of popular culture as produced by corporate entrepreneurs at the turn of the millennium. Nevertheless, I do argue that students need to be given credit for the very substantial cultural investment they have made in texts that do not necessarily meet every teacher's standard of what is worthwhile. Furthermore, students not only need to be acknowledged for what they have learned about their own contemporary culture, but also need to be offered ways of extending and refining their skills. And therein lies the rub. How do teachers extend and refine skills, strategies, and background understandings that may far exceed their own?

DEVELOPING CRITICAL STRATEGIES

What kinds of critical strategies do adolescents need to develop in order to make sense of the cultural world they inhabit? The narrative-based computer game and the popular movie are cultural texts that are often rendered more or less invisible in English classrooms, dismissed as collections of clichés and stereotypes. Yet large numbers of students come into class with substantial expertise with one or both of these formats, and it is difficult to argue that they are culturally and educationally insignificant. Today's students are often polyliterate with a very broad repertoire of skills and strategies that cover a wide range of media.

To explore the question of how teenagers develop expertise in the processing of such texts, I turn to a model of print reading based on a study of a thousand adolescents. Jack Thomson's (1987) model of how teenagers learn about reading is a useful contribution to this kind of discussion on several levels. He explicitly describes this outline as a developmental model. This dynamic approach has the potential to offer useful pointers to an exploration of secondary students' developing grasp of textual processing in other media as well as in print. Thomson's grid elucidates territory already familiar to many teachers and may serve as a helpful guide to areas not yet so well charted. As an extra advantage, it offers insights into reading processes that may be clear to teachers but present real barriers to some students.

Thomson posits a six-stage development process for response to literature (see Figure 8.1). It is fascinating to compare his schema to processes of critically comprehending texts in media other than print. The overlaps are illumi-

Figure 8.1. Developing a Response to Literature (from Thomson, 1987)

Process Stages: Kinds of Satisfaction	Process Strategies
1. Unreflective interest in action	a. Rudimentary mental images (stereotypes from film and television) b. Predicting what might happen in the short run
2. Empathizing	c. Mental images of affect d. Expectations about characters
3. Analogizing	e. Drawing on the repertoire of personal experience, making connections between characters and one's own life
4. Reflecting on the significance of events (theme) and behavior (distanced evaluation of characters)	f. Generating expectations about alternative possible long-term outcomes g. Interrogating the text, filling in gaps h. Formulating puzzles, enigmas, accepting hermeneutic challenges
5. Reviewing the whole work as the author's creation	i. Drawing on literary and cultural repertoires j. Interrogating the text, filling in gaps k. Recognition of implied author
6. Consciously considered relationship with the author, recognition of textual ideology, and understanding of self (identity theme) and of one's own reading processes	l. Recognition of implied reader in the text, and the relationship between implied reader m. Reflexiveness, leading to understanding of textual ideology, personal identity, and one's own reading processes

nating; perhaps even more fascinating are the stages where the different media part ways.

Naturally, no such simple grid can truly comprehend the complexities of the reading process. Nevertheless, it serves as a useful guide to exploring elements of reading, viewing, and interacting with computer texts, and offers the extra advantage of providing some sense of progression. Its very schematic nature opens the door to ways of talking usefully about text processing in different media.

Stage 1. Unreflective Interest in Action

There are those who would argue that the processing and enjoyment of computer games and Hollywood movies stops at Stage 1, with simple unreflective interest in action. Such a response overlooks the degree to which initial encounters with a text in any medium may baffle one observer while seeming utterly transparent to another. Stephen Heppell (1993) usefully describes this discrepancy with relation to computer games.

> When we adults observe children playing computer games, what we see is colored by our own experience. Our experience does not usually include computer games in any depth. We find a cacophony of sound, an anarchic blur of vision and action. We see children reacting to this, absorbed in their activity, but we under-value what is happening because we don't see what they see. They see sophisticated cues and clues. They see categories of visual information. They have expectations about the behaviour of objects on the screen, and within this environment they see challenges and solve problems that their parents and teachers are not even aware of.
>
> This is no different to the way in which a sophisticated reader sees books differently from a non-reader. To a non-reader, a library is a confusion of books, unstructured, chaotic. For teachers and parents, with a long history of familiarity with books and libraries, the same shelves hold past memories: Fiction, Romance, Reference, Travel and so on. The books are familiar friends and they can be referred to in conversation with other literate adults. (p. 3)

It takes time and experience to work out what needs attention in any form of text. Nobody can record and recollect every single detail, so even to engage in unreflective interest in action involves elements of intelligent selection of what to attend to and how to attend to it. Teachers who struggle with the opening complexities of a computer game may benefit from pausing to reflect that the early pages of an unfamiliar style of novel may seem just as confusing to an inexperienced reader. Learning to respect the complexity of something you already understand well is a process with many side benefits, not least for teaching.

Stage 2. Empathizing

Thomson (1987) places empathy early in the process of response to literature, but there are other ways of identifying with a text than the purely empathetic. The movie *Men in Black* is an interesting example of a case where viewers are invited to identify more with a point of view than with a particular character. The movie is a parody of many different genres: the rookie-veteran buddy show, the alien–science fiction show, the special effects–superhero show. There is hardly an element in the entire movie that is not a stereotype borrowed from another genre. Viewers are invited to enjoy their own recognition of these stereotypes and to develop their expectations about characters out of their knowledge of such stereotypes rather than by any engagement on the level of one complex human being to another.

Similarly, *Starship Titanic* operates on the basis of spoof, using many elements both of the *Titanic* story and of any number of generic sci-fi traditions to create a complicated story world. All the characters, other than the player of the game, are robots whose circuitry has been damaged by the crash of the spaceship, who have probably never had many qualities inviting human empathy, and who have now certainly lost those which they might have once had.

Empathy is an important element in engaging with stories, but it is not the only route into a story. Humor, which works very successfully in both these examples, provides another hook. The counterexamples of *Men in Black* and *Starship Titanic* provide useful reminders that teachers sometimes may presume on the replicability of their own experiences. Empathy is valued highly by most teachers of literature; adolescent readers may have priorities they value higher, but this does not mean they are unskillful.

Stage 3. Analogizing

Both *Men in Black* and *Starship Titanic* provide a reminder that analogizing can work more broadly than would seem to be the case in Thomson's schema. Texts can not only be related to life, they can also be related to other texts. Connections between texts, or *intertextuality*, is an important element of reading or viewing or interacting, and many contemporary texts work in this way. Quite young students, watching *The Simpsons* for example, know that many remarks, quips, even plotlines are completely referential to an outside text, even if they cannot identify the exact connection.

The ability to pick up such fleeting references is one of the credentials necessary to function in a postmodern culture, and it would not be too hard to picture a young person who arrived at the ability to develop such analogies well in advance of the ability to empathize. A reading-viewing-playing history that traveled through Saturday morning cartoons (most of which are highly referential) to *The Simpsons* to a movie like *Men in Black* would place a much higher premium on cleverness than on empathy and engagement. Thomson may be betraying a humanist bias in his listing, or it may be that his schema, based as it is on work done in the early and mid-1980s, reflects the priorities of a different time (not only precomputer but also, for the most part, prevideo tape).

Alternatively, it may be that the empathy-analogy axis works differently for reading than for viewing and playing. Movies can involve a very high degree of empathy and engagement, but they can also be slick and cool and very superficial in their affective connection. Computer games are largely deficient when it comes to empathetic hooks; they work on a much more intellectual basis. The 12-year-old who told me that *Myst* was not really a story, it was much more like a puzzle, may have been commenting indirectly on this feature of the narrative computer game. Technological priorities still dominate computer-based stories, and it may well be that empathy never becomes a strong feature in this kind of storytelling simply because the parameters of the exercise have to be so firmly laid down. Affective engagement seems to be much more powerful in other forms of computer text such as the online interactive fictional sites of MUDs and MOOs, in which participants have much more freedom to lay down their own controls and constraints for the fictional exercise.

Stage 4. Distanced Evaluation of Themes and Characters

Thomson appears to be discussing a progression through empathy to a more reflective and distanced form of consideration. I suspect that what antagonizes some English teachers who value such a progression very highly is the suspicion that some of their students are progressing to the stage of detachment without ever traveling through empathy. The kind of clever shallowness that predominates in much of contemporary culture (including *Starship Titanic*, *Men in Black*, and *The Simpsons*) actually devalues empathy as a purposeful strategy. Young people (and it may be that boys are more likely to follow this trajectory) may appreciate large swaths of current culture without ever placing any kind of emotional or strategic value on empathy. It would be possible for these same students to arrive at a similar devaluation of empathy by way of a route composed entirely of books, but it does seem rather less likely.

Stage 5. Reviewing the Whole Work as the Author's Creation

"All media are constructed" is the slogan of the media studies movement. Ironically, the medium where the constructed nature of the artifact is hardest to perceive is the book. The very industry that I described above, giving vast quantities of background information and supplying interviews with all the different creators at every level of the text, makes it very difficult for a contemporary student to avoid knowing that the movie *Men in Black* is a construct. Even students who take only a casual interest in the entertainment industry are unlikely to avoid every single element of the flood of background information that accompanies the release of a major film.

The kind of information made available by the movie industry is limited, however, and there is room for some interesting inquiry that takes students' basic understandings of the constructed nature of the story and pursues a broader and more critical approach. The example of *Men in Black* provides an interesting issue for discussion. In many texts, the story is the driving force that shapes the final product; in the case of *Men in Black*, the special effects were the dominant ingredient. In the early stages of developing the story and the special effects for the production, a successful puppet appealed to director Barry Sonnenfeld who immediately made changes in plot and characters to place this puppet in a more prominent role. The story was then developed around the new scenario (Key, 1997, p. 24). What does this say about the priorities of the movie world? Does it matter? Why or why not? There are many questions arising from this small fact, which is freely available in the public domain.

Indeed, it may be that teachers can make use of their students' broad familiarity with the decision-making processes of moviemaking. Classes may move more successfully into discussing some of the priorities in the composition of a novel after they have talked about similar stages in the making of a movie. Students who draw on their own recreational interest in the making of movies they have enjoyed may be surprised to discover how many of the same ideas make sense when thinking about the construction of a book. At the same time, students may learn to be more critical of and thoughtful about the information they are given as part of the marketing support of a new movie release.

Stage 6. Awareness of Relationship to Author and Ideology of Text, Understanding of Self, and One's Own Reading Processes

Thomson's final category is a complex one, and not surprisingly many of the young readers he surveyed had not yet reached this stage of self-awareness. Indeed, many adult readers pass relatively successful reading lives without ever coming to terms with the ideological implications of the texts they read.

Clearly, there is nothing about this stage of text processing that needs to be confined to books. Issues of detachment and reflection need not stop simply with print reading. The idea of teasing out the ideological elements at work in *Starship Titanic* is intrinsically interesting. According to Margaret Meek, every story is a "little theory of culture" (quoted in Brennan, 1999, p. 26), and the stories that appear on screens of one sort and another are no exception.

Similarly, there are questions to be raised concerning processing. In the little workroom scene at the start of this chapter, it was clear to everyone in the room that Jack had come up with a useful approach to the tantalizing and aggravating text of *Starship Titanic*. It was not necessary to be an expert to see what he was gaining through his expert shortcuts. Similarly, it would not be necessary to be an expert to ask what he was losing by this strategy. He was avoiding frustration; was this short-circuiting the experience of the game in some way? His skill led him to develop a reading of the text that was quasi-linear in its purposefulness; was he losing out on some of the joys of meandering within the text? It doesn't necessarily matter what the answer to this question is. Whatever his final judgment on this issue, Jack might benefit from being led to consider his strategies in a more reflective way, and it would not require an expert to lead him.

What it would require is time, space, and inclination to pay careful and respectful attention to what it is that Jack and his classmates are accomplishing in their engagements with media other than print. It would require opportunities to explore what it is that they do well and to find ways of drawing connections to activities they may be less adept at. It would call for teachers to make room for a class full of students with varying levels of skill and understanding. It is a complicated challenge, but we live in complicated times. The rewards of exploring the complexities of literate responses in many media will be great, and the necessity to address the real needs of our polyliterate students is undeniable.

SOME STRATEGIES

Acknowledging the complexity of the textual world in which today's students and teachers move is easy enough. Determining how to incorporate this understanding into teaching is a more complex question.

A useful first step would be for teachers (practicing or preservice) to explore their own expertises. A self-study of one's own media habits can be surprisingly illuminating: How many continuing stories from television series do you carry in your head at one time? How do you keep them straight, especially if you watch reruns as well as new segments and how does new information affect the way you interpret the old? What does watching such programs contribute to your understanding of the interpretation of fiction in general? What kinds of computer experience do you have in the run of an average week? Do you just send e-mails or surf the Web? Do you always use your computer in a purposeful way, or do you use it to have fun or just waste time? What do these experiences contribute to your imaginative and social life? What is the role of voluntary reading in your daily or weekly life? Do you stop reading in termtime because of other pressures, and if so, what does this fact tell you about your priorities? Do you read for escape, for self-improvement, for literary refreshment—or all of the above at one time or another? Do you ever experience books in other forms—on the radio or audiotape, as a movie or television adaptation? What are your views on these versions? Do you pay attention to all the different forms of "The Making of . . ." one movie or another? If you do, how does that information affect the way you watch the movie? How much rereading, rewatching, replaying do you do? Does your capacity to enjoy a reengagement with an already known text differ from one medium to another? For example, would you never read a book twice but happily watch a movie many times, or vice versa?

Simply thinking about one's own behaviors, habits, and strategies can expand the way one approaches other readers, viewers, and players in a classroom. The value of this self-study can be increased many times if there is a chance to compare one's own experiences with those of others, a useful exercise for a preservice education class or for a group of working teachers. The range of ways in which people take account of stories and other texts in many formats and media is startlingly large, and no one approach is necessarily the only or the right one.

Similarly, some form of this kind of self-exploration can be a very useful exercise in an English classroom, especially in the early stages of getting to know a class. It can be extremely helpful to get some idea of what expertise and understanding students bring into the classroom. A side benefit is that students may come to feel that what they do already know is being taken seriously. It is also useful for students as well as their teachers to gain some true understanding that there are many valid ways to approach a text. Encouraging students to keep a media diary, to compare and contrast their habits and behaviors with classmates in a small group, and to look at some of the broader implications in a whole-class discussion is an activity with much to recommend it. (If the groups are self-selected, students will feel happier about trading experiences, and it is also likely to increase the differentiation between groups, which may help to enrich the subsequent whole-class discussion.)

It is important not to make preassumptions about what will be revealed by students in such an exercise. I asked the students in the research project I described at the beginning of the chapter (then in Grade 5, Grade 8, and Grade 11) to keep such a diary. Despite my determination not to leap to conclusions in anticipation of the results, I found I was surprised to see how many of these students were committed to daily reading as well as watching television, listening to the radio, and messing around on the computer.

It is also important to find ways to stretch students beyond their present assumptions and to enable them to make some of their tacit understandings more explicit. One possibility is to compare and contrast adaptations. A comparison of a single scene from the movie version of *Men in Black* with the print versions in novel, novella, picture book, comic book, and screenplay would be an interesting exercise, and one that could be done with any number of popular movies. What makes one version work better than another? What decisions did different authors and/or producers make, and which ones were successful and why?

Students can also discuss the implications of the blanket marketing that accompanies the release of popular texts of various kinds (and again, it is important not to overlook print as an important part of the cultural matrix). This is a subject in which they have accumulated much experience, but they may well not have given the question of tie-ins and reproductions much *critical* thought.

A collection of samples of merchandise, television and Internet backup texts, and rewrites associated with a particular current story can prove illuminating to everybody.

There are many ways to tap into the understanding of students and to improve their capacity to look critically at the culture that surrounds them. It is important to respect what it is they bring to the exercise and vital not to take their recreational pleasures and simply turn them into fodder for school exercises. With care and attention, however, everyone can benefit from addressing the questions of what students know already and how they can be led to a more critical understanding.

REFERENCES

Brennan, G. (1999, January 8). English is . . . what exactly? *Times Educational Supplement*, p. 26.

Heppell, S. (1993, June 18). Hog in the limelight. *Times Educational Supplement*, pp. 3–4 (Computer Supplement).

Key, M. (1997, August/September). Rick Baker, man in black. *Make-Up Artist Magazine, 8,* 21–45.

Thomson, J. (1987). *Understanding teenagers' reading: Reading processes and the teaching of literature.* Melbourne: Methuen Australia.

CHAPTER 9

Words and Windows: Using Technology for Critical Literacy

ROBERTA F. HAMMETT
Memorial University of Newfoundland

Think about the literacy of romance for a minute. It used to be that lovers wrote notes or letters, exchanging news and expressions of love, when they were apart. We read such letters published in books like *Letters of Love and Duty: The Correspondence of Susanna and John Moodie* (Ballstadt, Hopkins, & Peterman, 1993) and *Love Across the Color Line: The Letters of Alice Hanley to Channing Lewis* (Lefkowitz-Horowitz & Peiss, 1996). Current media portray very different modes of communication between couples, and often in the process dramatize how new technologies have redefined the literacies and media of love and courtship. *You've Got Mail* (Ephron, 1999) helped us all fall in love with e-mail romance. Every major Internet communications provider has a "love and personals" site; on Classmates.com "hundreds of people have reconnected with their high school sweetheart" (PR Newswire Association, 2002). Chat rooms, electronic mail, and radio phone-in shows remind us that communication media, along with the skills of communicating, have changed.

We can use Internet technologies to meet, court, and even marry one another. During my dissertation study, one of the guest speakers, Juanita,[1] told the young women participants in my computer camp about her AOL romance that resulted in bills of $500 a month (before the days of more reasonable Internet access providers). She said, "I met somebody in one of the chat rooms, and we got involved romantically. I had a PowerBook at home that slept with me. So I would wake up at two or three in the morning and turn the computer on and see if I had a message from him. So it's very addictive. But I'm past that stage now" (Hammett, 1997, p. 59).

The camp participants, exploring the Internet, located and played with the

Cyrano Server, which invites visitors to submit various bits of information that "Cyrano" then uses to compose and send a love letter to the recipient of one's choice. As the site introduction says:

> Want to tell someone how you feel, but are shy and unimaginative? Cyrano is here to write your love letters for you. If you already know the perfect words to say, then you can write the letter yourself. Either way, Cyrano will email the recipient of your letter to let him or her know how you really feel. (http://www.nando.net/toys/cyrano.html)

It wouldn't take very long with an Internet search engine for me to find a story (perhaps the one I heard on the radio the other day) about an Internet wedding—whether in an online newspaper archive or on a personal Web site. I'll save that work for another day and get to my point.

These examples of new technologies, conventions, and literacies used for romantic purposes illustrate that there are ways of communicating our thoughts, desires, cultures, and identities that require English language arts teachers to teach different content, different ways, and different tools. Trend (1997) highlights the changing literacies when he says, "Young people are alienated by the disparity between the type of literacies sanctioned in school and the literacies they practice in their daily lives" (p. 139). In response to changes in media and messages and to altering entertainment preferences of the students we teach, new Canadian curricular documents like APEF (Atlantic Provinces Education Foundation, 1996) and WCP (Western Canadian Protocol for Collaboration in Basic Education, 1998) are redefining literacy, texts, and goals. Similarly, the United Kingdom, Australia, New Zealand, and the United States are redesigning curricula to recognize that media and technology figure ever more prominently in the lives of students we teach, and that the nature of English language arts (ELA) instruction and curricula needs to expand to incorporate the forms, genres, conventions, and structures of a wider variety of texts.

RETHINKING DEFINITIONS OF LITERACY

The new Canadian curricular documents, responding to redefinitions of literacy in the popular media and information technology, are expanding the notions of literacy in the ELA classroom. The APEF (1996), for example, tells us that

> what it means to be literate will continue to change as visual and electronic media become more and more dominant as forms of expression and communication.

As recently as one hundred years ago, literacy meant the ability to recall and recite from familiar texts and to write signatures. Even twenty years ago, definitions of literacy were linked almost exclusively to print materials. The vast spread of technology and media has broadened our concept of literacy. To participate fully in today's society and function competently in the workplace, students need to read and use a range of texts. (p. 1)

Although I do not particularly endorse the role of schools as preparing students to "function . . . in the workplace," as APEF states, I do believe that reading the world is as important as reading the word, to paraphrase Freire (Freire & Macedo, 1987, pp. 30–32), and I believe it is important to prepare students to be informed citizens who read media and other texts competently and critically, for social and political purposes.

Similarly, the *Standards for the English Language Arts* sponsored by National Council of Teachers of English (NCTE) and International Reading Association (IRA) state as Standard 1: "Students read a wide range of print and non-print texts to build an understanding of texts, of themselves, and of the cultures of the United States and the world; to acquire new information; to respond to the needs and demands of society and the workplace; and for personal fulfillment" (NCTE-IRA, 1996).

As members of a global society at the beginning of the twenty-first century, we have come to expect that information will be shared with us through a wide variety of media—billboards and bus boards, television programs of all kinds, license plates, computer programs, Web pages and other Internet sites and technologies, newspapers, magazines, memos, signs, tabloids, graffiti, digital signboards, skywriting, and on and on. New technologies' impact on mass communication media is highly familiar to us as citizens.

In response, curricular foundation documents also expand definitions of texts. The APEF (1996) notes:

In this document, the term text is used to describe any language event, whether oral, written, or visual. In this sense, a conversation, a poem, a novel, a poster, a music video, a television program, and a multimedia production, for example, are all texts. (p. 1)

The NCTE-IRA Standard 6 states: "Students apply knowledge of language structure, language conventions (e.g., spelling and punctuation), media techniques, figurative language, and genre to create, critique, and discuss print and non-print texts" (NCTE and IRA, 1996).

These documents, as should be expected when our North American world runs on technology, indicate that our students should learn to use technology "to meet their own information needs" (APEF, 1996, p. 40). Standard 8 says explicitly: "Students use a variety of technological and information resources (e.g., libraries, databases, computer networks, video) to gather and synthesize information and to create and communicate knowledge" (NCTE-IRA, 1996). This chapter will demonstrate how, within a critical pedagogy, a variety of computer technologies can be used to achieve some of the outcomes defined in each of the documents.

NEW TECHNOLOGIES

Most of my research in using new technologies for knowledge construction and literacy learning, including media literacy, has been with secondary English education students. My colleagues and I have asked our students to consider the usefulness of computer technologies in teaching English language arts by experiencing those possibilities themselves. I will provide brief descriptions of some of these enterprises here, and then provide further brief descriptions of some of the actual products later in this article.

One of the experiences asked of our students was to discuss texts and issues and ideas on electronic bulletin boards or asynchronous Web conferences. These conferences have centered on the assigned course texts, around topics related to course issues that arise in the news media, and in response to concerns students observe and experience in the schools in which they are visiting. Web conferences generally involve a student raising a question or issue for discussion with some explanatory comment, and other participants contributing to any particular thread of conversation that appeals to them. In high schools, such conversations might be initiated in relation to media or other texts students are studying as individuals, small groups, or as a class. One common text or multiple texts with similar themes or other commonalties might form the basis for the Web conference. Critical dialogue, of the kind advocated by Shor and Freire (1987), can be encouraged by interventions by the teacher. My observation, confirmed by students in research and yet to be reported, is that students who feel unable to contribute to such conversations in class feel more able to do so on the electronic bulletin board.

Another assignment for our students was to conduct book inquiries through e-mail transmissions. Rather than sharing ideas orally with all of their classmates, small groups of students were encouraged to discuss a number of books on a theme (reading theory or portfolio assessment, for example). In our education class, these inquiry discussions sometimes led to a class presentation by the inquiry group. Again, I suggest this activity is appropriate for high school ELA students.[2] A teacher could provide online suggestions to students engaged in the literature study groups like those Cherland (2000) describes.

We also asked students to compose Web pages that represent knowledge, ideas, readings of texts, and challenges to an Internet audience. Using the composing features of browser software (like Netscape Communicator) or using other Web-authoring software (available as freeware on the Internet or purchased online or in local computer stores), students quickly learned to create Web pages. These Web pages, as well as sharing students' perspectives, invited debate and response from others, thus stimulating further reflection.

Finally, we asked students to compose several different multimedia projects.[3] Using a variety of software, students were able to learn quickly how to digitize audio, video, and images; create digital movies from scanned images and digitized audio; replace the sound track of a digitized videoclip with a different audio track; manipulate and change existing images; and combine any and all of these products with print text in a hypertext program. These hypermedia were composed to represent readings of and reactions to *text sets*, which are a variety of books on related themes read by individuals or small groups (see Hammett, 1999a; Short, 1992); to explore media representations (see Hammett, 1999b; Myers, Hammett, & McKillop, 1998); and to represent meanings of classic texts like Shakespeare's Romeo and Juliet (see Hammett, 1999a). In hypermedia, not only can a number of different media be combined in one space or window, but also hyperlinks between spaces can take readers-viewers instantly to related sites. Several spaces can be kept open on the computer screen so that several different texts can be viewed together. This juxtaposing of texts invites discussion of the questions, challenges, and conflicting views they represent individually and in relation to one another.

In addition to the computer technologies discussed above, there are other technologies already familiar to teachers in schools: cassette recorders, school PA systems, radio broadcasting booths, video cameras and VCRs, and computer desktop publishing programs that produce newspapers, brochures, and magazines. All of these media permit students to represent and share ideas, knowledge, and identities. And all of them can be used within a critical pedagogy to achieve the outcomes envisioned in the ELA curricula.

CONSTRUCTING KNOWLEDGE

The education students who worked together to create the *Romeo and Juliet* hypermedia demonstrated how this technology facilitates knowledge construction (Bonk & Cunningham, 1998; Vygotsky, 1978). By gathering together a variety of media culture texts on related themes (suicide, first love, parent-child conflicts, despair, and so forth), the students were constructing knowledge about those themes and about Shakespeare's play. Hypermedia, which allows several texts to be available or open on one screen, makes explicit the connections between ideas. Rosenblatt (1978) declares, "We are not usually

Figure 9.1. Despair Windows (Storyspace: Eastgate Systems, Inc. http://www.eastgate.com)

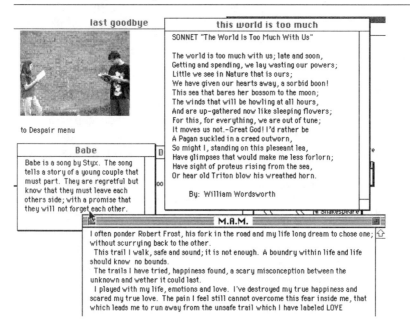

aware of the organizing or constructive process—the fitting together and interpretation of visual clues—which results in the act of perception" (p. 50). Similarly, we are not always concretely aware of the previous readings, events, and experiences that we bring to a "new" text in order to make meaning of it.

This intertextuality is made explicit in hypermedia, as Figure 9.1 illustrates. In the graphic, several Storyspace[4] windows are open; in each window several different texts are displayed: print text (the Wordsworth sonnet), the student's personal reflection, an introduction to the Styx (1987) song "Babe," and the digital movie that shows scenes of ninth-grade students reading *Romeo and Juliet*. The sound track is the Styx song: "Babe I'm leaving / I must be on my way . . . / I'll be missing you."

These textual explorations of various moments of despair lead the students to an understanding of the Shakespeare text. Although, in composing hypermedia, they start with the Shakespeare text and bring in the media culture texts to illustrate it, in reading *Romeo and Juliet* they bring understandings formed in multiple experiences with media culture to the classic text. In the Suicide strand of the hypermedia, clips from several videos and quotations from poems, novels, and songs illustrate this: *My Darling, My Hamburger* (Zindel, 1969), "How Did You Die?" (Edmund Vance Cook, in Fellerman, 1936),

"Grind" (Alice in Chains, 1995), *Dead Poets Society* (Weir, 1989), and several other texts have provided the students with understandings of suicide. (See Hammett, 1999a, for more detailed descriptions and discussion of this hypermedia.) Similarly in the Balcony, First Love, and Parental Conflict strands, popular culture texts demonstrate the variety and number of perspectives on the themes shared in songs and films that students bring to their reading of Shakespeare.

Hypermedia facilitates knowledge construction in another way as well. Students may learn firsthand about the construction and manipulation inherent in media texts. Combining scanned images and digitized audio tracks (including their own tape-recorded commentaries), students create digital movies. They also use image software to scan, crop, and manipulate images, including their own digital photographs; they use sound software to digitize, crop, and change audio; and they use video software to work with videoclips. In composing the *Romeo and Juliet* hypermedia, students learned how movie sound tracks affect and change the mood, reactions, and meanings of the visual images and scenes. They experienced the effects they can create in viewers when they replaced, with several different songs, the original sound track of Juliet's funeral scene in Zefferelli's (1968) movie version of the play. "Grind" (Alice in Chains, 1995) and "Girlfriend in a Coma" (The Smiths, 1987), when used as sound tracks for the scene, seemed to completely change our reaction and interpretation. Our attention was focused on different visual images, and the visual images appeared to be different (movement seemed faster, and so on). By constructing these effects themselves, students will have a more practical understanding of how professionals achieve the effects that move their audiences.

These are a few illustrations of the constructivist possibilities of hypermedia and other technologies. As others have argued, computer technology supports learning in a variety of ways that empower students as producers of knowledge (Jonassen, 1996; Jonassen, Peck, & Wilson, 1999; Spender, 1995). It can also support learning within a critical perspective.

CRITICAL PEDAGOGY

Although not receiving the explicit attention warranted, critical pedagogy and literacy are included in new ELA curricular documents. The NCTE-IRA *Standards* suggest, "Students participate as knowledgeable, reflective, creative, and critical members of a variety of literacy communities" (NCTE, 1996). There is little explicit explanation of or reference to critical literacy activities, though they are loosely implied in some standards.

The APEF includes a section on equity and diversity that tells teachers that the curriculum must do the following:

> . . . Students need opportunities to
>
> • Critically examine different experiences and perspectives within social and cultural contexts
> • Examine ways in which language and images are able to create, reinforce, and perpetuate gender, cultural, and other forms of stereotyping and biases
> • Use their own voices to understand, shape and share their worlds. (p. 42)

There are other challenges to teachers within the realm of critical literacy and pedagogy included in the document. I have selected three, which I use here to introduce three possibilities for critical literacy in schools. In relation to each, I will provide some theoretical framework and then describe how computer technologies can and have been used to achieve these critical literacy goals.

The APEF and WCP use the phrase "writing and other ways of representing" to suggest, among other meanings, that a variety of technologies and kinds of texts can be created to convey ideas, responses, knowledge, and understandings. The NCTE-IRA *Standards*, while not using the word *representation*, refer to similar activities in phrases such as "use spoken, written, and visual language" (NCTE, 1998, Standard 12). I'll focus on the word *representing*. The texts we read and create are about representation—representation of identities, meanings, values, experiences, ideologies, and cultures. All communications, whatever their form or medium, are about engaging with others as social beings. Thus our engagement with others' texts is, in effect, a process of understanding their representations and making them meaningful to ourselves. Much of current Canadian and U.S. teaching practice builds on the reader-response theory of Louise Rosenblatt (1938/1983; 1978), inviting readers to respond aesthetically and personally to texts, representing their own reactions and connections in dialogue and through various technologies.

The students in our classrooms represent an ever-widening variety of worlds. In large comprehensive schools students come together from many communities, bringing with them many cultures, including media culture. And this latter culture is as real and important to many of our students as ethnic, regional, and national cultures. Our task is to help our students read all those texts more critically and to understand how representations are mediated. To accomplish this, we may acquaint them with the conventions of various media (see, for example, Teasley & Wilder, 1997, on film), involve them in semiotic analyses of signs and their iconic, indexical, and symbolic meanings (see Myers, Hammett, & McKillop, 1998, on hypermedia), engage them in hermeneutic circle readings (Llewelyn, 1985) of all kinds of texts and their conventions, and challenge them with deep viewing of television programs and commercials (see Watts-Pailliotet, 1999). Any and all of these activities are appropriate and worthwhile; nonetheless, I would like to have students move beyond the reading, however critical, of existing texts to the generation of new ones. Computer technologies can be used by students to manipulate existing texts in ways that offer them up for closer examination and ways that create new texts.

DIFFERENT EXPERIENCES AND PERSPECTIVES

Greenlaw (2000) discusses the use of the Internet to access, deliberate about, and research multicultural and world literature within a critical pedagogy. My colleague Barrie R. C. Barrell and I (Hammett & Barrell, 1999; Barrell & Hammett, 2002) have also used the possibilities of Internet technologies to encourage secondary English education students to represent their cultural identities and resistant readings to E. Annie Proulx's (1993) novel *The Shipping News*. In a site entitled *Newfoundlanders Read The Shipping News* (http://www .educ.mun.ca/educ4142/index.html), the students shared their reactions—not always favorable—to the novel; interpreted and explained different passages; provided additional information; and represented their own identities, cultures, and communities to illustrate or challenge various themes and ideas in the novel.

Such generative processes as the construction of Web pages in response to readings of other texts involve students in "critically examin[ing] different experiences and perspectives within social and cultural contexts" (APEF, p. 42). In their *Shipping News* Web pages, students explored connections between a variety of texts, building an intertext that exposes ideas, representations, readings, and reactions for critique. By publishing their work (and their identities) on the Internet, and by inviting responses, the students are potentially discovering how their texts affect an audience. They are engaging in a unique social and cultural experience. It is social at the point of creation, as the students work collaboratively on the class Web site to represent readings that are themselves social engagements (with E. Annie Proulx and her text participants or characters), and at the point of publication, as students add their e-mail addresses to invite response and post their pages on the World Wide Web. It is also critical in the sense that students adopt subjective rather than objective positions in relation to texts; that they intervene in, interpret, and reinterpret texts; and that they contest the positions and ideologies offered by texts. Students learn that experience is mediated by authors of print and other media texts, and they learn that they too can mediate their own and others' experiences. These are some aspects of critical literacy as I define it; others will follow.

EXAMINING BIASES AND STEREOTYPES

Another aspect of critical literacy and pedagogy is the close examination of representations, particularly of race or ethnicity, class, age, and gender representations. Students are often encouraged, particularly in media literacy units, to examine advertisements, films, television programs, and other media (including print) texts to compile images of women or particular racial groups. This kind of examination of media texts can be facilitated with computer technology, as the following examples illustrate. In their critique of media representations of race, class, age, and gender, the education students used multimedia technologies in interesting ways. One product, for example, combined a series of digitized images (from news magazines and other sources) of Native American females: Disney's *Pocahontas* (Gabriel & Goldberg, 1995), two seventeenth-century portraits of Pocahontas, cherubic "Indian" children with feather headdresses in a picture on a wall, and finally a contemporary image of a young Native American girl sitting on a couch. These images, sound tracked with Peter Gabriel's (1990) song "Shaking the Tree," were interset with carefully chosen transitions, part of the Adobe Premiere software. Another similar digital movie created by the students presented a wide variety of images of women, considered by the composers to be both positive (a woman aged 101) and negative (the *Little Mermaid*) to Madonna's words, "Express yourself, don't repress yourself" (1990). The students intended that these images, presented in such close juxtaposition, would contrast one another and thus raise questions about how women are often represented in media as young, beautiful, White, and sexy. By including both a picture of the first Barbie and Disney's Pocahontas in the series of images, they pointed out how Disney had commodified all women, including the "real" Pocahontas.

Students find these computer activities pleasurable and exciting, and willingly engage in an examination of *their* media. Oftentimes their compositions are not explicitly critical and political (see Myers, Hammett, & McKillop, 1998; Hammett, 1999a). On those occasions, the teacher can use the hypermedia that students have created to engage the class in critical discussion and dialogical teaching—a process that, as Shor and Freire (1987) explain, creates and re-creates the self, exposes ideas for examination, stimulates one's own and others' thinking, evokes new meanings and possibilities, reinterprets, and challenges. Urged to uncover the underlying ideologies and values in media texts, students should both realize the role of media in their self-construction and become more critical consumers of all texts.

UNDERSTANDING, SHAPING, AND SHARING THEIR WORLDS

The third of the quoted APEF directions, which I recognize as the Freirean sense of critical literacy, urges that students "use their own voices to understand, shape, and share their worlds" (p. 42). Freire (1970/1992; 1973/1994) and his followers (McLaren & Lankshear, 1994; Shor, 1992; Taylor, 1993; and many others) argue that literacy learners should be offered opportunity and assistance in reading, discussing, and writing their own worlds and lived experiences. A political goal of conscientization is achieved as learners—collaboratively and individually—recognize oppressions. They also acquire and use literacies to name the world, that is, to write and thus transform it (Freire, 1970/1992). In classrooms, we may engage students in discussion, in "critical and liberating dialogue" (Freire, 1970/1992, p. 52), as discussed above. And we encourage them to publish texts that use writing and other ways of representing to "celebrate and build community" (WCP, p. 9); to "explore thoughts, ideas, feelings and experiences" (p. 65); and to share cultural and other identities (p. 114). My example of the *Shipping News* Web site, described above, demonstrates this objective. Lewis (1995) provides us with another fine example. His students at Jimmy Sandy Memorial School in the "isolated sub-Arctic" (p. 30) community of Kawawachikamach, Quebec, used Internet, multimedia, and other technologies to collect and audiotape, write, illustrate, and publish community legends and stories, thus preserving Neskapi traditions and cultures.

By assembling and transmediating their own, their families', and their communities' stories, experiences, and histories, students will not only recognize oppressions but also assume an empowering and empowered role in their mediation. They will recognize the role of literacies in social action as they engage in projects of possibility (Simon, 1987) that may transform their worlds.

CONCLUSION

Some of the English teachers I talk with express the fear that the new ELA curricula, with their emphases on viewing, others ways of representing, and technologies, will result in students who cannot express themselves; indeed, who turn to the Cyrano Server to write imaginative love letters for them and who communicate by e-mail or in chat rooms, using emoticons like :) to represent emotion, and refusing capitals, correct punctuation, and other conventions of writing in e-mail communications. Although many of the computer-assisted projects I have described above involved the digitizing of audio, visual, and video texts, all of them also involved reading and writing print texts. The "other" media texts are almost always contextualized and explained in print texts in hypermedia composing.

Studying media and using new technologies should pose no threat to traditional literacies of reading and writing. As I have demonstrated and as new Canadian and U.S. curricula have recognized, the study of all these texts and literacies can be integrated to both complement and challenge one another. The critical study of mass communications (newscasts and even movies like *You've Got Mail*) and personal communications (like e-mail transmissions) can lead naturally from and to the critical study of essays, novels, and other genres, as well as it leads to the deconstruction of sonnets and letters, the technologies of love and personal communication of another day. A hypermedia project about Shakespeare's *Romeo and Juliet*, such as the one a group of our education students composed, can lead to the critical exploration and understanding of contemporary media culture and values as well as Elizabethan culture and values. Additionally, students can be asked to interrogate their readings of all the texts, to discuss the values and assumptions that privilege some texts over others, and to analyze the ideologies inherent in the texts themselves.

Students use hypermedia, other computer technologies, and media texts very enthusiastically to express or represent their ideas and knowledge. All of the students with whom I have worked on computer-generated texts, including desktop publishing, have labored extra hours to create the texts and the special effects they envision. Such assiduity and enthusiasm among students further convinces me that broadening the range of texts and the definitions of literacy and creating those six curricular strands of speaking and listening, reading and viewing, and writing and other ways of representing is a step in the right direction by the APEF and WCP. If we teachers of English language arts take advantage of opportunities for critical pedagogy presented by media and technologies and the pleasures they offer students, we can achieve some important educational outcomes, envisioned not only by authors of curriculum but also by important liberatory educational theorists like Paulo Freire.

NOTES

1. A pseudonym.

2. A word about availability of technology here: We should not assume students have home computers—an assumption that privileges some students over others. Special times could be designated in computer rooms to address equity issues (see Hammett, 1997). On the other hand, we can expect more personal computers in all schools and homes in the future. I am suggesting activities that could make use of whatever technology is available, possibly currently unused by ELA teachers. Once they become knowledgeable about possible activities, teachers will be better able to select and order

hardware and software that will encourage students to be producers rather than consumers of knowledge.

3. Because I encourage students to freely use and digitize any available media texts, the resulting projects should not be published on the Web. Multimedia projects, created collaboratively or individually by students, can be demonstrated to classmates for study and entertainment. They can be used, as I am suggesting in this chapter, as jumping off points for critical dialogue about the messages and other aspects of media.

4. Storyspace is a multimedia composing program available from Eastgate Systems, 134 Main Street, Watertown, MA 02472 (http://www.eastgate.com/Storyspace .html).

REFERENCES

Alice in Chains (Cantrell, J.). (1995). Grind. On *Alice in Chains* [CD]. Nashville, TN: Columbia Records/Tripod.

Atlantic Provinces Education Foundation (APEF). (1996). *English language arts foundation*. Halifax, NS: Author.

Ballstadt, C., Hopkins, E., & Peterman, M. (Eds.). (1993). *Letters of love and duty: The correspondence of Susanna and John Moodie*. Toronto: University of Toronto Press.

Barrell, B., & Hammett, R. (2002). A critical social literacy project: Newfoundlanders challenge *The Shipping News*. *Interchange, 33*(2), 139–158.

Bonk, C. J., & Cunningham, D. (1998). Searching for learner-centered, constructivist, and sociocultural components of collaborative educational learning tools. In C. J. Bonk & K. King (Eds.), *Electronic collaborators: Learner-centered technologies for literacy, apprenticeship, and discourse* (pp. 25–50). Mahwah, NJ: Erlbaum.

Cherland, M. Rogers. (2000). Teaching beyond reader response: Reading the culture to know the self. In B. Barrell & R. Hammett (Eds.), *Advocating change: Contemporary issues in subject English* (pp. 104–116). Toronto: Irwin.

Ephron, N. (Director). (1999). *You've got mail* [Film].

Fellerman, H. (1936). *The best loved poems of the American people* (reissue). New York: Doubleday.

Freire, P. (1992). *Pedagogy of the oppressed* (M. B. Ramos, Trans.). New York: Continuum. (Original work published 1970)

Freire, P. (1994). *Education for critical consciousness*. New York: Continuum. (Original work published 1973)

Freire, P., & Macedo, D. (1987). *Literacy: Reading the word and the world*. South Hadley, MA: Bergin & Garvey.

Gabriel, M., & Goldberg, E. (Directors). (1995). *Pocahontas* [Videotape]. Burbank, CA: Buena Vista Home Video.

Gabriel, P. (1990). Shaking the tree. On *Shaking the tree: Sixteen golden greats* [CD]. Los Angeles: Uni/Geffen.

Greenlaw, J. (2000). Negotiating cultural identities on the internet. In B. Barrell & R. Hammett (Eds.), *Advocating change: Contemporary issues in subject English* (pp. 147–160). Toronto: Irwin.

Hammett, R. (1997). *Adolescent women, identity, and hypermedia composing.* Unpublished doctoral dissertation, Pennsylvania State University, College Park.

Hammett, R. (1999a). Girlfriend in a coma: Responding to literature through hypermedia. In P. Mosenthal & A. Watts-Pailliotet (Eds.), *Reconceptualizing literacy in a new age of media, multimedia, and hypermedia* (pp. 105–127). Greenwich, CT: JAI Press.

Hammett, R. (1999b). Intermediality, hypermedia, and critical media literacy. In L. Semali & A. Watts-Pailliotet (Eds.), *Intermediality: Teachers' handbook of critical media literacy* (pp. 306–328). Boulder, CO: Westview Press.

Hammett, R., & Barrell, B. (1999) Resistance and re-representation as reflection. *English Education, 31*(3), 248–254.

Jonassen, D. (1996). *Computers in the classroom: Mindtools for critical thinking.* Englewood Cliffs, NJ: Merrill/Prentice-Hall.

Jonassen, D., Peck, K., & Wilson, B. (1999). *Learning with technology: A constructivist perspective.* Englewood Cliffs, NJ: Merrill/Prentice-Hall.

Lefkowitz-Horowitz, H., & Peiss, K. (Eds.). (1996). *Love across the color line: The letters of Alice Hanley to Channing Lewis.* Amherst: University of Massachusetts Press.

Lewis, D. (1995, March). Making the community connection. *The Computing Teacher, 22,* 30–32.

Llewelyn, J. (1985). *Beyond metaphysics? The hermeneutic circle in contemporary continental philosophy.* Atlantic Highlands, NJ: Humanities Press International.

Madonna. (1990). Express yourself. On *The Immaculate Collection* [CD]. Burbank, CA: Wea/Warner Brothers.

McLaren, P., & Lankshear, C. (Eds.). (1994). *Politics of liberation: Paths from Freire.* New York: Routledge.

Myers, J., Hammett, R., & McKillop, A. M. (1998). Opportunites for critical literacy and pedagogy in student-authored hypermedia. In D. Reinking, M. McKenna, L. Labbo, & R. Keiffer (Eds.), *Handbook of literacy and technology: Transformations in a post-typographic world* (pp. 63–78). Mahwah, NJ: Lawrence Erlbaum.

Myers, J., Hammett, R., & McKillop, A. M. (2000). Connecting, exploring and exposing self in hypermedia projects. In M. A. Gallego & S. Hollingsworth (Eds.), *What counts as literacy: Challenging the school standard* (pp. 85–105). New York: Teachers College Press.

National Council of Teachers of English (NCTE) and International Reading Association (IRA). (1996). *Standards for the English language arts.* Urbana, IL, and Newark, DE: Authors.

PR Newswire Association. (2002, February 12). National survey finds almost 40% of those polled have used the Internet to look up or reconnect with a high school flame. (http://www.prnewswire.com)

Proulx, E. A. (1993). *The Shipping News.* New York: Simon & Schuster.

Rosenblatt, L. (1978). *The reader, the text, the poem: The transactional theory of the literary work.* Carbondale: Southern Illinois University Press.

Rosenblatt, L. (1983). *Literature as exploration* (4th ed.). New York: Modern Language Association. (Original work published 1938)

Shor, I. (1992). *Empowering education: Critical teaching and social change.* Chicago: University of Chicago Press.

Shor, I., & Freire, P. (1987). *A pedagogy for liberation: Dialogues on transforming education.* Granby, MA: Bergin & Garvey.

Short, K. (1992). Making connections across literature and life. In K. Holland, R. Hungerford, & S. Ernst (Eds.), *Journeying: Children responding to literature* (pp. 284–301). Portsmouth, NH: Heinemann.

Simon, R. (1987). Empowerment as a pedagogy of possibility. *Language Arts, 64*(4), 370–382.

The Smiths. (1987). Girlfriend in a coma. On *Strangeways, here we come* [CD]. Burbank, CA: Wea/Warner Brothers.

Spender, D. (1995). *Nattering on the net: Women, power, and cyberspace.* North Melbourne, Australia: Spinifex Press.

Styx. (1987). Babe. On *Cornerstone* [CD]. Nashville, TN: Pgd/A&M.

Taylor, P. (1993). *The texts of Paulo Freire.* Buckingham, UK: Open University Press.

Teasley, A., & Wilder, A. (1997). *Reel conversations: Reading films with young adults.* Portsmouth, NH: Heinemann.

Trend, D. (1997). *Cultural democracy: Politics, media, and new technology.* Albany: State University of New York Press.

Vygotsky, L. S. (1978). *Mind in society: The development of higher psychological processes* (M. Cole, V. John-Steiner, S. Scribner, & E. Souberman, Eds.). Cambridge, MA: Harvard University Press.

Watts-Pailliotet, A. (1999). Deep viewing: Intermediality in preservice teacher education. In L. Semali & A. Watts-Pailliotet (Eds.), *Intermediality: Teachers' handbook of critical media literacy* (pp. 31–51). Boulder, CO: Westview Press.

Weir, P. (Director). (1989). *Dead poets society* [Film]. Los Angeles: Touchstone Pictures.

Western Canadian Protocol for Collaboration in Basic Education (WCP). (1998). *The common curriculum framework for English language arts, kindergarten to grade 12.* Edmonton: Alberta Education.

Zefferelli, F. (Director). (1968). *Romeo and Juliet* [Film]. Los Angeles: Paramount Pictures.

Zindel, P. (1969). *My darling, my hamburger.* New York: Bantam Books.

CHAPTER 10

Context, Text, and Tests: Issues in English Assessment in the United States

SARAH W. BECK
New York University

Educators distinguish between two types of assessment: *formative* and *summative*. These different types require teachers to assume different roles: Formative assessments cast them as a facilitator or coach; summative assessments, as an examiner or judge. This long-standing theoretical and practical tension has been exacerbated in recent years as policy makers and school administrators have placed increasing emphasis on the summative purpose of assessment, which has cast the interests of this group in opposition to the interests of teachers. While teachers mainly value assessment as a means toward improving their teaching and students' learning, test designers, school administrators, and policy makers care mainly about the capacity of an assessment to regulate teachers and render them accountable.

Can any assessment ever satisfy both sides or serve both purposes? This conundrum underlies the questions that I take up in this chapter. My perspective is sociocultural, and one of its central assumptions is that education, as broadly conceived, must address two sometimes competing goals: the development of the individual and the maintenance of the culture (Wells, 1993). The tools of culture include spoken and written language used for the range of functions that Britton, Burgess, Martin, McLeod, and Rosen (1975) identified: transactional, expressive, and poetic. Three decades ago, using these broad categories, they discovered that school writing in the secondary grades was most frequently limited to the transactional, and since then circumstances appear to have changed little, suggesting that our culture—at least as schools conceive of it—places a higher value on the use of print as a tool for conveying information and articulating ideas.

The concept of authenticity—a shibboleth in the rhetoric of assessment in the late 1980s—is a useful one for understanding the intersection between individual and cultural development in the sociocultural paradox of education's goal. *Authentic* can mean closer alignment of assessment practices in reading and writing with the practices of real-world specialists; it can also imply a holistic view of the learner that values formative over summative assessments (Beck, 1999). With respect to literacy development, English teachers are caught in a paradox: They must encourage the development of students' individual voices and interpretive stances as writers and readers while at the same time ensuring that students are prepared to reproduce those textual forms, or genres, that serve as passports to the more privileged tiers of our society.

The title of this chapter encapsulates this paradox. So-called advances in standardized testing in the past 2 decades have attempted to provide a richer context for the production and comprehension of texts by including more open response questions, which in theory provide students with greater latitude in bringing the "context of the mind" (Cazden, 1982) to bear on their reading and writing in response to questions. However, judgments about students' performance on these standardized tests inevitably privilege text over context, convention over creativity. When the text is at the center of a writing assessment, the evaluator focuses on the degree to which the student's writing matches criteria for a successful production, and the judgment of a match or mismatch with the target performance can be made more reliable if teachers are trained in identifying these criteria. When assessment methods acknowledge context, however, there are complicating factors: the student's prior history as a writer, the teacher's understanding of what the student is capable of based on her observation of this prior history, and the ways in which the instructional context may have facilitated, or inhibited, the student's writing performance. This text-context distinction applies to reading as well. Emphasis on text in the assessment of reading comprehension implies that the meaning is in the text as packaged and interpreted by test designers—New Criticism revisited. An alternative approach to judging students' reading would be to consider the legitimacy of an interpretation as informed by the context of both the reader's prior reading history and by ongoing classroom discussion—by the "discourse community" (cf. Brodkey, 1987) consisting of a student's teacher and peers. Much of the disagreement between those who value teachers' knowledge above all else in measuring students' performance and those who support the efforts of standardized test designers could be said to hinge on this issue of context.

INFLUENCES ON ASSESSMENT PRACTICES

Essential to any discussion of assessment in English education is a discussion of standards. Although standards in themselves usually have little import for teachers other than through the assessment tasks they spawn, contrasts among standards are worthy of study in themselves to the extent that they illustrate differences in how we articulate the literacy tools and practices deemed most necessary for succeeding in our culture. The development of learning standards for students in grades K–12 inevitably sparks ideological controversy, regardless of whether professional groups such as the National Council of Teachers of English (NCTE) or federal or state governments sponsor their development. For example, a joint effort between the International Reading Association (IRA) and the NCTE to develop standards for the English language arts required three attempts before a final document materialized (NCTE/IRA, 1996). Moreover, the term *standards* itself is an ambiguous one, so much so that parties with widely divergent ideological and practical concerns are able to interpret and manipulate the term to serve their own ends (see Mayher, 1999, for a thorough review of this issue). The concept of standards has been invoked for purposes such as promoting an elite work force for a capitalist economy, ensuring equal opportunity for students from all sectors of society, and for denigrating the professional judgment of teachers. These conflicting agendas, rather than the standards themselves, are what exert the primary influence on assessment practices at the state, district, and classroom levels.

The business world appears to have an increasing influence on standards construction. The rhetoric about standards frequently speaks to the economy's need for workers who possess complex critical thinking skills rather than teachers' need to develop and exercise their professional knowledge (Murnane & Levy, 1996; Resnick & Wirt, 1996). If cultural reproduction is one of education's two competing goals as seen from a sociocultural perspective, then what is the engine that drives this reproduction? In a former era, English teachers' notions of high literary culture or mastery of classical rhetorical forms may have set the standards. Today, however, cultural reproduction is at least partly synonymous with economic productivity. The textual forms that students are expected to produce and interpret frequently evoke the realm of functional, workplace literacy. For example, a recent edition of the Stanford 9 Achievement Test featured a job application as one of the reading passages, followed by comprehension questions. One way of resolving the sociocultural paradox is to assume that in today's capitalist economy individual development entails the pursuit of economic success in an environment that ostensibly facilitates such success by providing equal opportunities for all students.

The recurring theme of expectations for literacy performance in the future workplace is also evident in appeals for students to develop strategic critical thinking skills that are transferable across subject domains. This concern is more than a response to pressure from the business world—after all, the crystal ball that permits education reformers a glimpse into the society of the future has yet to materialize. It also reflects a shift toward constructivism as the dominant theoretical model informing current thinking about education (Calfee, 1994). This shift is reflected in an increase in open-ended questions to supplement multiple-choice items on standardized tests and a concomitant shift toward the use of writing to measure students' capacity for thought. The range of what students are expected to do with texts has increased, and an ability to answer multiple-choice tests on literary passages no longer guarantees one's achievement of high school–level standards of literacy, though this ability remains a basic necessity for academic success. The demands of these more complex tasks require English teachers who prepare students for these assessments to understand how the activities of reading and writing can mutually support each other. Such assessments also undercut the long-held assumption that literature constitutes the primary subject matter in the English classroom. Now students must read and understand informational as well as literary texts and be able to compare texts to others through a variety of interpretive lenses. They must also write in the analytic and argumentative modes and draw the content of their writing from multiple sources, including oral ones.

STATEWIDE ASSESSMENTS IN NEW YORK AND MASSACHUSETTS

A comparison between ELA assessments from two states, New York and Massachusetts, illuminates differences in education policy makers' expectations for English students and in how those expectations align with current speculation about the literacy skills that students will need in order to contribute to a capitalist economy. The standards with which these assessments are aligned also suggest important differences, the most obvious being a difference in relative emphasis on context or text. The New York standards emphasize the context of use for texts, stating for example that "students will collect data, facts, and ideas; discover relationships, concepts, and generalizations; and use knowledge generated from oral, written, and electronically produced texts" (New York State Board of Regents, 1996, p. 7). This standard distinguishes between types of cognitive processes—discovering relationships, making generalizations, and analyzing experience—that a reader applies to a text. In Massachusetts, by contrast, the Language, Reading, and Literature Strand specifies separate standards for the reading of different genres such as poetry, drama, myth, fiction, and nonfiction—a classification system that emphasizes form over function and minimizes the differences in function between such genres as personal essays, newspaper editorials, and political speeches (Massachusetts Department of Education, 2001). And the recurring refrain, "students will provide evidence from the text to support their understanding," which appears in six of the eleven standards within the Language, Reading, and Literature Strand, suggests that the standards architects in Massachusetts are more preoccupied with the notion of the text as the center of meaning than their counterparts in New York. Form appears to take precedence over function, and text over context, in Massachusetts's vision for students' competence in English.

Standards, of course, affect instruction only insofar as they are manifest in state assessments. Systematic research has confirmed what teachers already know through experience: The requirements of standardized high-stakes tests have a greater impact on teaching and learning than the frequently richer and more comprehensive curriculum frameworks with which such standardized tests are supposedly aligned (Hillocks, 2002).

Recent items from the New York State Regents Exam illustrate an intersection of reading, writing, and listening, in a range of genres, that exemplifies a more integrated approach to assessment of skills and a closer alignment between the kinds of texts that students are asked to read and those they are asked to write. For example, one question on the first part of the Comprehensive Examination in English on a recent administration of the test specifies a particular rhetorical situation before asking students to listen to a television broadcast about the influenza epidemic of 1918, and then to "write a position paper for your social studies class, in which you argue that World War I may have contributed to the spread of the influenza epidemic of 1918" (New York State Board of Regents, 2002a, p. 2). Another question requires a similar kind of performance—a persuasive essay for participation in a hypothetical debate team—but based on written rather than spoken sources of information. Both prompts on this part of the test specify a particular rhetorical situation, requiring students to present themselves in a role that they would not typically occupy within the parameters of a more traditional English class, that is, as students of social studies and science. This feature of the test speaks to the relevance of English as a domain that extends across subject areas in the high school. The second part of this test requires students to read texts about the nature of time that are written in two different genres—narrative and informational—and to draw on both in constructing an analytical response in the form of "a unified essay about the nature of time" (New York State Board of Regents, 2002c, p. 2).

The Regents approach to English assessment thus measures students' knowledge about a range of written genres as well as their ability to process language in different modes. It also implicitly demonstrates a view of English as a subject that should be assessed holistically, through the demonstration of interrelated skills, rather than independently. They integrate these skills by dividing the writing and reading tasks into three separate categories, each task graded with its own rubric. These categories are "Listening and Writing for Information and Understanding" (2002b, p. 3), "Reading and Writing for Information and Understanding" (2002b, p. 52), and "Reading and Writing for Literary Response" (2002d, p. 3). The division of tasks in this way suggests three underlying assumptions about the nature of literacy: (a) In today's society oral texts are as important a source of information as printed ones; (b) writing is a measure of understanding and not just of technical mastery of forms and conventions; and (c) "literary response" entails a stance toward text that differs in identifiable ways from the stance one assumes when reading "for information," as in Rosenblatt's (1978) distinction between "aesthetic" and "efferent" reading.

The three different rubrics used to score each item suggest some features that distinguish what is expected of students in each of the three different literacy tasks. For example, in the two "writing for information and understanding" tasks, the student is supposed to "make insightful connections between information and ideas in the documents [or texts] and the assigned task," whereas in "writing for literary response" the student is supposed to "make insightful connections between the *controlling idea* and the ideas in each text." In the "information and understanding" tasks, the rubric's focus is on the rhetorical situation, emphasizing audience and purpose, whereas in the "literary response" task the focus is on the "controlling idea" through which the writer is supposed to link multiple literary texts. Though the rubric for all three writing activities on this assessment is divided into the same general domains—Meaning, Development, Organization, Language Use and Conventions—variations in each rubric in the domains of Meaning and Development reflect an assumption that there are differences in the discourse knowledge and cognitive processes entailed in each activity. Nevertheless, a common criterion in all three rubrics is the use of textual evidence to support the student writer's ideas: "the extent to which ideas are elaborated using specific and relevant evidence from the text(s)" is an important feature in distinguishing between a high- and low-scoring essay on all prompts (Rubric for Session Two, Part A—Scoring Rubric for Reading and Writing for Literary Response). Thus, in order to write successfully across all three prompts, students must not only be able to adjust the language and structure of their essays to particular purposes and audiences, they must also demonstrate the ability to identify salient information in the texts provided and incorporate that information into elaborated pieces of writing.

The rubrics' recognition that features of writing differ depending on audience and purpose supports the prompts' detailed specifications for context, though the meaning of *context* is somewhat different in each of the writing tasks. In the first two prompts the emphasis is on writing to fulfill a social purpose, whereas in the third prompt the emphasis is on writing to illustrate how the writer has formed a unique interpretation of the commonalties between the two literary texts. Whereas the "assigned task" comes from the social context, the "controlling idea" emerges from the reader's transaction (cf. Rosenblatt, 1978) with the two texts. Also implicit in the design of this assessment is the notion that reading literature is a private, personal activity, while reading or listening to informational texts is a public one. In both cases the prompt implicitly acknowledges that what the student produces in writing is the product of an interaction between context and text—either the rhetorical context of the communicative situation (student to peer audience) or the internal context of the reader's mind. What does this acknowledgment mean for the balance between individual development and cultural continuity? To accommodate context as an influence in the analysis of text is to promote adaptability to context in learners who prepare for the test. Though this might not lead to personal growth in the sense of self-discovery or self-expression, it at least gives students social, cultural, and economic advantages to better prepare them for success in the current economy. The trajectory of individual development here is more toward citizenship than personal fulfillment.

By contrast, the English/Language Arts section of the Massachusetts Comprehensive Assessment System (MCAS) appears to ignore the role of context in shaping a reader's interpretation of a text or analysis of information. Nor does it acknowledge that forms of written discourse differ depending on the intellectual processes they represent. There is only one opportunity for extended writing (i.e., longer than a paragraph) on the MCAS, and for several years the genre of that writing has been the literary analysis essay,[1] which the most successful students typically render in five-paragraph form. It could be argued that this genre is related to other kinds of academic writing that sociocultural theorists have characterized as representing a capacity for abstract thought (Applebee, 1984; Olson, 1977). And the literary analysis essay has traditionally been one of the "genres of power" (Lemke, 1988) that are crucial to students' school success (Christie, 1986) and that permit access to higher education and future economic benefits. Though one can find counterparts to the thesis-support structure of written argument in a range of types of writing in academic disciplines, the structural form of the five-paragraph essay bears little resemblance to written genres that actually accomplish the work of any professions. Thus, ironically, the test prompt encourages students to make connections between literature and life in their thinking about literature by introducing the prompt with the phrase "In literature, as in life . . ." at the same time that they are writing in a genre that fulfills no obvious function other than reproducing a highly conventionalized form of writing that is peculiar to school culture. While two of the three writing tasks on the Regents Exam specify a particular audience and function designed to be relevant and appealing to teenagers, the Massachusetts prompts make no such specifications. It is assumed, then, that the purpose and audience for this writing task are the traditional ones: writing in order to be evaluated by the teacher (cf. Britton et al., 1975).

The MCAS English exam does require students to incorporate close readings from text and to articulate the results of their textual analysis in writing, but in short answers rather than in an extended essay. Moreover, in the MCAS the activities of writing and reading are not integrated to the same extent that they are in the New York assessment. This lack of integration is evident in the division of the ELA MCAS into two sections: "Language and Literature," and "Composition." In the former, writing serves the sole purpose of measuring the depth of students' understanding of a topic the test designers have deemed essential to the passage. For example, after reading an autobiographical passage, "Easy Job, Good Wages" by Jesús Colón, that recounts the writer's disillusionment with his first experience working as a manual laborer, students are asked to respond to the following question:

> How does the meaning of the expression, "Easy job, good wages," change for the author from the beginning of the story to the end? Use information from the story to support your answer. (Massachusetts Department of Education, 2002a)

This question constrains students' reading of the passage to focus narrowly on what the title means and, further, how this meaning changes over the course of the passage. Indeed, repeating the phrase and related key words, and using temporal markers to suggest change or development, seem to be sufficient for a high-scoring response, as this top-scoring example from the set of benchmark responses suggests (italic type marks words or phrases that repeat the language of the question):

> The term *"Easy Job, Good Wages" changes* the authors feelings about the job *from the beginning of the story to the end. In the beginning of the story* the author was just simply looking for any job of any sort. The author doesn't realize that the literal *meaning of "Easy Job, Good Wages"* is very deceiving to the reader. Once the author acquires the job and does the actual job the author realizes the true *meaning* of the expression. At the *end of the story* the author simply smiles an ancient, tired, knowing smile. This means that the author won't fall for catchy phrases like the previous one for the job of picking labels off of glass bottles with your thumb until it bleeds and almost lose your thumbnail. (Massachusetts Department of Education, 2002b)

The student who produced this passage has obviously learned the trick for succeeding on this type of short-answer test: Repeat the language of the question in your answer, and you will get a high score. To be sure, it is easier for a teacher to identify and explicitly teach students the kind of reading skills that will enable them to succeed on this kind of task than it is to prepare them for a unified essay in which they must develop their own controlling idea about two different literary works, as the Regents Exam asks them to do. Yet writing such limited, repetitive responses will do little to enlarge students' capacities as readers of literature.

This test's limited conception of what constitutes a written response to literature is also evident in the rubric that is used to score the one opportunity that the MCAS offers students to write an extended analysis of a literary work, on the "Composition" section of the test. This rubric makes no reference to the activity of reading or literary response, defining the characteristics of highest scoring essays about literary characters as simply "rich topic/idea development," "careful and/or subtle organization," and "effective/rich use of language." The cost-efficiency of such a rubric is obvious—it can be applied across tasks, thus eliminating the need to train scorers on multiple rubrics. Yet it ultimately inhibits teachers' and students' recognition of the fundamental differences in rhetorical and cognitive processes that different literacy tasks entail. In the Regents Exam, by contrast, a separate rubric for written literary response suggests that the test designers view writing about literature as a specialized mode of discourse (cf. Beach, 1999; Christie, 1986).

To sum up, New York's Regents English Exam, in contrast to its MCAS counterpart, more aptly reflects pressure to align expectations for student work in school with the future expectations of the workplace as well as with current theories of cognition. This assessment expects students to know about and be able to write in a wider range of genres that more closely reflect the skills needed in the real world, and demands more extensive writing as a measure of comprehension and interpretation. In theory, then, preparing for the Regents Exam offers a wider range of opportunities for the individual student to develop a repertoire of proficiency with the cultural tools of written and spoken texts than does the MCAS. Although the Regents test does not measure students' capacities as writers of expressive or poetic language—the rubric clearly states that purely personal responses will earn a student no more than a zero— the passages selected as reading and listening prompts suggest that teachers should incorporate a wider range of texts into their reading curriculum.[2]

The shift toward a more inclusive view of text that is evident in the New York Regents Exam holds the potential to address a long-standing paradox in English instruction and assessment: While students typically read genres in the poetic mode, most of the writing assigned to them is in the transactional mode (Britton et al., 1975)—most frequently the five-paragraph theme about literature. Traditional English instruction requires students to produce a genre of writing that they rarely read or critique and to study genres that they are only infrequently asked to imitate. We need a closer alignment between texts that students read and texts that they write and a greater range of possibilities across different text types.

At the same time, however, the influence of policy makers concerned about students' preparedness for the world of work has meant that in choosing between developmental and normative assessment, between formative and summative, schools and districts are leaning increasingly toward the latter. This is not to say that student-centered forms of assessment have disappeared altogether from the literacy landscape. However, the locus of control for these student-centered methods has shifted to the school or even classroom level, becoming the province of individual teachers and usually taking a back seat to the requirements of large-scale assessments (see Koretz, 1998, for an illuminating history of the portfolio initiative in Vermont, which exemplifies this shift).

WHAT ARE ENGLISH TEACHERS TO DO?

English teachers must be mindful of education's two competing aims: the development of the individual and the development of the culture. Within the context of English education, *the development of the individual* refers to the acquisition of the linguistic and literary knowledge that will promote a student's cognitive, social, and moral development such that she will be able to fully participate in society (cf. Coles, 1990; Kilpatrick, Wolfe, & Wolfe, 1994), but not at the expense of her sense of self. Essential to this definition is the idea of text as a tool for cultural participation (Olson, 1995) as well as for individual development. However, tests that require students to articulate their understanding of a literary text in the textually explicit style of "essayist literacy" (Farr, 1993; Olson, 1977) disadvantages students whose cultural, linguistic, or socioeconomic backgrounds place them outside the mainstream of educational practices. Such students may be more comfortable responding to literature in an oral, field-dependent (Smitherman, 1977) mode than in the textually explicit "essayist" manner of writing. For these students, acquiring mainstream discourse practices in speech and in writing entails a loss of cultural affiliation as well as a loss of individual voice, and thus the sacrifice—and the potential for resistance—is greater than for students from mainstream discourse backgrounds. Because tasks on standardized tests do not acknowledge the similarities between such oral, field-dependent discourse styles and conventional forms of literary reasoning and analytical thinking (as demonstrated, for example, in Farr, 1993, and Lee, 1995), it is left to the teacher to help students figure out how to move from one discourse style to another.

Only multiple sources of data can tell an evaluator whether a student's acquisition of literacy is sponsoring his development as an individual, through cultivation of a personal voice in writing or of original critical perspectives on literature, while simultaneously promoting his understanding of how to interpret and produce culturally powerful text genres. And the only evaluator in a position to obtain such data is a teacher. When standardized assessments restrict students' opportunities to demonstrate their full capacity to respond to literature or write meaningful prose, how can English teachers ensure that their curricula and instruction are not similarly restrictive? One solution incorporates tasks and criteria that align standardized assessments into a more comprehensive classroom assessment system. Lucy Calkins and her colleagues at Teachers' College (Calkins, Montgomery, & Santman, 1998) have proposed such a compromise, applying their well-established cooperative strategies for literature instruction to the teaching of test-taking techniques.

While Calkins's approach to preparation for standardized literacy assessments suggests how to incorporate test preparation into instruction, other educators have developed systems for classroom assessment that are comprehensive enough to record students' progress toward mastery of test-related skills at the same time that they capture more sophisticated levels of literacy and language development. The American Literacy Profile Scales (Griffin, Smith, & Burrill, 1995) provide a framework consisting of nine "bands" of competence ranging from emergent literacy to sophisticated analytical writing and sensitivity to the influences of writer, reader, and situation on text comprehension. Moreover, these profiles encompass the widest possible domains of knowledge and skill relevant to students' participation in an English classroom. In addition to writing and reading, they enable teachers to define students' capacities in speaking, listening, and viewing. Offering a detailed description of the kinds of skills that students are expected to master within each band, these profiles could be adapted to highlight those strategies and areas of competence that are most frequently measured on standardized tests. For example, one of the writing bands specifies the ability to "develop analytical arguments" (p. 52) while the corresponding reading band assesses the ability to "read beyond literal text and seek deeper meaning" and "relate social implications to text" (p. 32). These skills are clearly relevant to the tasks cited above from the New York exam and even from the more limited Massachusetts exam. Though intended for use by a classroom teacher, these profiles contain criteria that correspond to the expectations of the architects of state assessments. Thus local and large-scale assessments need not work at cross-purposes.

Indeed, the skills described in the profiles are more advanced, more rigorous, than those required on many state assessments. Writing Band I, for example, includes among its competencies whether a student can use analogies, symbolism, irony, and elaborated metaphorical language in writing—all skills commonly evident in published or professional writing but bearing little apparent utility for the workplace of the future and therefore not figuring prominently in the priorities of state-level test designers. Students from cultural backgrounds with rich oral traditions may be able to demonstrate this high-level literacy skill even if they fail to "write paragraphs to develop [a] logical sequence of ideas" (p. 49), a competence located lower on the Profile Scales. The advantage of the Literacy Profiles, as an assessment instrument, is that their comprehensiveness allows teachers to capture a holistic picture of students' capabilities, while the division of performance into different skill areas allows students as well as their teachers to identify students' strengths and shortcomings more precisely than a simple letter grade or numerical score permits.

Nancie Atwell's approach to assessing her students' writing offers a similarly optimistic set of possibilities for reconciling socially constructed criteria for the evaluation of writing with a student-centered approach to assessment. All students begin the year with the same general goals that Atwell derives from the common practices of adult writers, but as the year progresses Atwell designs individual goals *for* and *with* each individual student. For Atwell, teaching students to evaluate their own writing should serve the larger goal of teaching them to be better writers: "The better our students become as evaluators of their writing and reading, the better their writing and reading will be" (1998, p. 327).

Atwell's philosophy of writing assessment reminds us not to lose sight of the larger purpose of assessment in the teaching of English: that it is a means to an end, not an end in itself. Although writing for self-expression and discovery, purposes cherished by the writing process movement of the 1970s and 1980s, seems to have taken a back seat to the more urgent purpose of writing for social advancement, we must remember that the purpose of measuring what students can do with language should not be to show what teachers and schools have accomplished with their instruction, but to show what progress students have made in becoming fully literate writers, readers, and speakers.

NOTES

1. Autobiography—an "expressive" form of writing—is the only other genre that has appeared on the writing portion of the MCAS, but this was before a passing score became a graduation requirement.

2. These more comprehensive characteristics aside, the quality of the reading selections on the Regents Exam is still in question. Several news stories have exposed censorship of potentially controversial elements from test passages (Winerip, 2003).

REFERENCES

Applebee, A. (1984). Writing and reasoning. *Review of Educational Research, 54*(4), 577–96.

Atwell, N. (1998). *In the middle: New understandings about writing, reading and learning* (2nd ed.). Portsmouth: Heinemann-Boynton/Cook.

Beach, R. (1999). Evaluating students' response strategies in writing about literature. In C. Cooper & L. Odell (Eds.), *Evaluating writing: The role of teachers' knowledge about text, learning and culture* (pp. 195–222). Urbana, IL: National Council of Teachers of English.

Beck, S. (1999). *A theoretical framework for authentic writing assessment and its relevance to writing assessment practices in secondary school classrooms.* Unpublished qualifying paper, Harvard Graduate School of Education, Cambridge, MA.

Britton, J., Burgess, T., Martin, N., McLeod, A., & Rosen, H. (1975). *The development of writing abilities (11–18).* London: Macmillan.

Brodkey, L. (1987). *Academic writing as social practice.* Philadelphia: Temple University Press.

Calfee, R. (1994). *Implications of cognitive psychology for authentic assessment and instruction* (Technical Report No. 69). Berkeley, CA: National Center for the Study of Writing.

Calkins, L., Montgomery, K., & Santman, D. (1998). *A teachers' guide to standardized reading tests.* Portsmouth, NH: Heinemann.

Cazden, C. (1982). Contexts for literacy: In the mind and in the classroom. *Journal of Reading Behavior, 14*(4), 413–417.

Christie, F. (1986). Writing in schools: Generic structures as ways of meaning. In B. Couture (Ed.), *Functional approaches to writing* (pp. 221–240). London: Frances Pinter.

Coles, R. (1990). *The call of stories: Teaching and the moral imagination.* New York: Mariner Books.

Farr, M. (1993). Essayist literacy and other verbal performances. *Written Communication, 10*(1), 4–38.

Griffin, P., Smith, P., & Burrill, L. (1995). *The American literacy profile scales: A framework for authentic assessment.* Portsmouth, NH: Heinemann.

Hillocks, G. (2002). *The testing trap: How state writing assessments control learning.* New York: Teachers College Press.

Kilpatrick, W., Wolfe, G., & Wolfe, S. (1994). *Books that build character: A guide to teaching your child moral values through stories.* New York: Touchstone.

Koretz, D. (1998). Large-scale portfolio assessments in the United States: Evidence pertaining to the quality of measurement. *Assessment in Education, 5*(3), 309–334.

Lee, C. (1995). A culturally based cognitive apprenticeship: Teaching African American high school students skills in literary interpretation. *Reading Research Quarterly, 30*(4), 608–630.

Lemke, J. (1988). Genres, semantics and classroom education. *Linguistics and Education, 1*(1), 1–99.

Massachusetts Department of Education. (2001, June). *Massachusetts English language arts curriculum frameworks.* Malden, MA: Author.

Massachusetts Department of Education. (2002a). *Massachusetts comprehensive assessment system: Release of spring 2002 test items.* Malden, MA: Author.

Massachusetts Department of Education. (2002b). *2002 MCAS sample student work and scoring guides.* Available http://www.doe.mass.edu/mcas/student/2002/

Mayher, J. S. (1999). Reflections on standards and standard setting: An insider/outsider perspective on the NCTE/IRA standards. *English Education, 31*(2), 106–21.

Murnane, R., & Levy, F. (1996). *Teaching the new basic skills: Principles for educating children to thrive in a changing economy.* New York: Free Press.

National Council of Teachers of English and International Reading Association. (1996). *Standards for the English language arts.* Urbana, IL, and Newark, DE: Authors.

New York State Board of Regents. (1996). *Learning standards for English language arts* (Revised Edition). Albany, NY: Author.

New York State Board of Regents. (2002a, August). *Regents high school examination: Comprehensive examination in English, session one.* Albany, NY: Author.

New York State Board of Regents. (2002b, August). *Regents high school examination: Comprehensive examination in English, session one—Scoring key and rating guide.* Albany, NY: Author.

New York State Board of Regents. (2002c, August). *Regents high school examination: Comprehensive examination in English, session two.* Albany, NY: Author.

New York State Board of Regents. (2002d, August). *Regents high school examination: Comprehensive examination in English, session two—Scoring key and rating guide.* Albany, NY: Author.

Olson, D. (1977). From utterance to text: The bias of language in speech and writing. *Harvard Educational Review, 47*(3), 257–281.

Olson, D. (1995). Conceptualizing the written word: An intellectual autobiography. *Written Communication, 12*(3), 277–97.

Resnick, L. B., & Wirt, J. G. (Eds.). (1996). *Linking school and work: The role of standards and assessments.* San Francisco: Jossey-Bass.

Rosenblatt, L. M. (1978). *The reader, the text, the poem: The transactional theory of the literary work.* Carbondale: Southern Illinois University Press.

Smitherman, G. (1977). *Talkin' and testifyin': The language of Black America.* Boston: Houghton Mifflin.

Wells, G. (1993). Reevaluating the IRF sequence: A proposal for the articulation of theories of activity and discourse for the analysis of teaching and learning in the classroom. *Linguistics and Education, 5*(1), 1–37.

Winerip, M. (2003, January 8). How New York exams rewrite literature (a sequel). *New York Times*, p. B7.

About the Contributors

Barrie R. C. Barrell is a Professor of English Education at Memorial University of Newfoundland. He recently edited the text *Technology, Teaching and Learning: Issues in the Integration of Technology* (Detselig, 2001). His previous edited books with Roberta Hammett include *Digital Expressions: Media Literacy and English Language Arts* (Detselig, 2002) and *Advocating Change: Contemporary Issues in Subject English* (Irwin, 2000). As well as being a visiting scholar at the University of Calgary in Alberta, he has taught at Bishop's University in Quebec and Mount Saint Vincent University in Nova Scotia.

Sarah W. Beck is an Assistant Professor of English Education at New York University and a former secondary school English teacher. She is the coeditor of *Perspectives on Language and Literacy: Beyond the Here and Now* (Harvard Educational Review, 2001). Her current research focuses on understanding and expanding the academic literacy practices of students in inner-city schools.

Maryann Dickar is an Assistant Professor of Teaching and Learning at New York University where she also serves as project director of the NYU Alternative Certification Initiative. Her scholarship focuses on issues in urban schooling, particularly student culture and its relationship to academic culture and school reform. She also is exploring the impact of race on schooling experiences of both urban teachers and students. Additionally, she has taught English and social studies in high schools in New York City.

Roberta F. Hammett is Associate Dean for Graduate Programs, Faculty of Education, Memorial University of Newfoundland. Her research interests include the literacy implications and applications of computer technologies, teacher education, and critical media literacy. She teaches courses in English education, technology integration, media literacy, feminist epistemology, and research methodology. She is currently at work on a coauthored book on identity and feminist pedagogies. Her recent publications include two coedited texts, *Digital Expressions: Media Literacy and English Language Arts* (Detselig, 2002) and *Advocating Change: Contemporary Issues in Subject English* (Irwin, 2000). Her World Wide Web address is http://www.ucs.mun.ca/~hammett/

Ursula A. Kelly is a Professor in the Faculty of Education at Memorial University of Newfoundland. She is the author of *Marketing Place: Cultural Politics, Regionalism and Reading* (Fernwood Books, 1993) and *Schooling Desire: Literacy, Cultural Politics and Pedagogy* (Routledge, 1997), as well as numerous journal articles and chapters in edited books. Her teaching, research, and writing interests are within cultural studies, literacies and language, and critical pedagogies.

Carmen Kynard is a doctoral student in English Education at New York University. She has taught in New York City high schools and at the City University of New York for 10 years and is currently completing her dissertation on the interrelationships among schooling, language, and literacy for African American students in the United States.

Margaret Mackey teaches at the School of Library and Information Studies at the University of Alberta, working in the field of young adult literature and researching the literate responses and behaviors of adolescents and children as they process texts in many different media. She has taught preservice and in-service English teachers, and was a school English teacher for 10 years. She is the author of many articles and a book entitled *The Case of Peter Rabbit: Changing Conditions of Literature for Children* (Garland Publishing, 1998).

Jill Kedersha McClay is an Associate Professor in the University of Alberta Faculty of Education. After graduating from the University of Pennsylvania, she began her career teaching high school English language arts in New Jersey and later in Mexico. She currently teaches language and literacy courses at the graduate and undergraduate levels, and her research focuses on writing theory and pedagogy. She has also coedited *Literary Experiences*, a widely used literature series for high school students.

John S. Mayher is Professor of English Education at New York University where he also serves as director of Teacher Education. He received the David Russell Award for Research in English Education from the National Council of Teachers of English for his book *Uncommon Sense: Theoretical Practice in Language Education* (Boynton/Cook, 1990) in 1992 and the Distinguished Service Award from NCTE in 1998. He was earlier the chair of the Conference on English Education and convenor of the Fifth Conference of the International Federation for the Teaching of English at New York University in 1995.

Robert Morgan is an Associate Professor in the Department of Curriculum, Teaching, and Learning at the Ontario Institute for Studies in Education, University of Toronto. His areas of research and teaching include media education, cultural studies, English in secondary schools, and questions about the educative dimensions of space and place. He has published articles in a variety of journals including *College English, New Education, Discourse, Journal of Educational Thought,* and *Continuum* and in international collections such as *Teaching Popular Culture* (D. Buckingham, editor) and *Teaching in Media* (A. Hart, editor).

Gordon M. Pradl is Professor of English Education at New York University. He is the author of *Literature for Democracy: Reading as a Social Act* (Boynton/Cook, 1996) and the editor of *Prospect and Retrospect: Selected Essays of James Britton* (Boynton/Cook, 1982). From 1985 to 1992, he served as the coeditor of *English Education,* the professional journal for the Conference on English Education.

John Willinsky is the Pacific Press Professor of Literacy and Technology at the University of British Columbia and has recently published *Learning to Divide the World* (University of Minnesota Press, 1998) and *Technologies of Knowing* (Beacon Press, 1999).

Index